Information Society and Media Development in Modern Mongolia

AF833615

Information Society and Media Development in Modern Mongolia

Undrah Baasanjav

Routledge
Taylor & Francis Group
LONDON AND NEW YORK

First published in 2025 by Amsterdam University Press Ltd.

Published 2025 by Routledge
4 Park Square, Milton Park, Abingdon, Oxon OX14 4RN
605 Third Avenue, New York, NY 10158

Routledge is an imprint of the Taylor & Francis Group, an informa business

© Author / Taylor & Francis Group 2025

All rights reserved. No part of this book may be reprinted or reproduced or utilised in any form or by any electronic, mechanical, or other means, now known or hereafter invented, including photocopying and recording, or in any information storage or retrieval system, without permission in writing from the publishers.

Trademark notice: Product or corporate names may be trademarks or registered trademarks, and are used only for identification and explanation without intent to infringe.

ISBN: 9789463729888 (hbk)
ISBN: 9781041181422 (pbk)
ISBN: 9781003697985 (ebk)
NUR 740 | 811

Cover illustration: photo taken in Bayankhongor province by Khurelbaatar Badamsuren

Cover design: Coördesign, Leiden

DOI: 10.5117/9789463729888

For Product Safety Concerns and Information please contact our EU representative:
GPSR@taylorandfrancis.com
Taylor & Francis Verlag GmbH, Kaufingerstraße 24, 80331 München, Germany

Table of Contents

List of Figures

Introduction

This book aims to provide evidence of informational society and media development in contemporary Mongolia, a thirty-three-year-old democracy. Mongolia is known in the West for its nomadic culture on the plateau of the Central Asian steppes and Chinggis Khan's empire in the thirteenth and fourteenth centuries. The Mongol Empire (1206–1338) created an effective pony express military communication system, which relied upon highly mobile messengers (*ulaach*) who galloped on horses from one node (*urtoo*) to another (Mayhew 2001). The nodes of the military intelligence system were *gers* (*yurt*), circular felt tents that are easily set up and dismantled. The *ger* remains home for nomadic Mongolian people even today, eight hundred years later, and the messaging system operated until the beginning of the twentieth century in Mongolia. After the collapse of Chinggis Khan's empire and its many subsequent kingdoms, Mongolia survived a three-century-long Manchu colonization (1691–1911), and a short period of independence under Bogd Khan (1911–21), after which it became the world's second socialist country (1921–90).

Since the collapse of the Soviet bloc in 1989, Mongolia has transitioned from a communist political system to a democracy and from a centrally planned economy to a market economy. Landlocked between China and Russia over its large 1.5 million square kilometer territory with a sparse population of 3.4 million, the country's contemporary information and media spheres have changed dramatically in the rapidly globalizing world. The geopolitical location, nomadic culture, recent communist history, and untapped natural resources are the contours and contexts that background this book, which examines the media and informational spheres of contemporary Mongolia in the twenty-first century.

In the years following the opening of the country from the Soviet bloc, media—from tweets to text messages, from television soap operas to advertisements in dramas—has grown rapidly in Mongolian and other languages. Mongolia's contemporary media environment is a mixed bag of old and new, foreign and traditional, and nostalgic and commercialized products. Entertainment products, from MTV to Korean soap operas and from American

Undrah Baasanjav, *Information Society and Media Development in Modern Mongolia*.
Taylor & Francis Group, 2025
DOI: 10.5117/9789463729888_INTRO

NBA games to Japanese sumo wrestling championships, have become the staples of cable and satellite channels in most homes in the cities, as well as in provinces (*aimags*). Over the last couple of decades, Mongolia has also drastically increased access to information and communication technology (ICT) for its population of 3.4 million, indicated by the numbers of mobile phone users (3.8 million), internet users (2.91 million), and Facebook users (2.1 million) (See figure 1.1). The explosion of the production of computers, microchips, and communication equipment in Taiwan, Singapore, and South Korea (known as Asian tiger economies), and recently China, spilled over to Mongolia, reducing the equipment prices of ICTs and increasing access to smartphones. Mongolia's 2.43 million smartphone users spend an average of seventy-seven minutes a day on Facebook (Munkhbaatar 2020). Owing to YouTube and social media campaigns, the Mongolian rock and metal band *Hu* reached seventy-three million views on YouTube as of April 2021, which is unprecedented in Mongolian cultural affairs (Farber 2019). This media flow undoubtedly shapes and influences the contemporary Mongolian identity. These dramatic changes in the informational sphere and the role of media and informational flow in contemporary Mongolian society and culture have yet to be studied in depth.

The term "media" for this book encompasses all types of traditional print and electronic media, as well as the internet and social media that are increasingly converged on digital platforms. Converged media is defined as "the coming together of all forms of mediated communications in an electronic, digital form driven by computers" (Pavlik 1996, 132). All forms of Mongolian media are created, produced, and distributed digitally, from text messages to tweets, from television shows on Netflix series to big- or small-screen advertisements. Boundaries between traditional media that were established during the socialist era and digital and social media that became prevalent in recent years have increasingly blurred within the context of dramatic economic and political changes in Mongolia. During the seventy years under socialism, the foundations of Mongolia's newspapers, radio, television, and journalism were molded, and the media served the purpose of propagandizing the population with the communist party's ideology and positively presenting socialism to mobilize the masses culturally.

The concepts of a free press and media operating in the marketplace of ideas and functioning as a watchdog institution are relatively new to Mongolia, and the continuity and disruption of the media in the last thirty-three years have occurred in radically different historical contexts, similar to other former socialist countries (Jakubowicz 2011; Richter 2011; Voltmer

2013). The path dependency of and nostalgia for the media systems that fostered communist political ideology continuously factor in the development of media in former socialist countries (Voltmer 2013). Former socialist countries in Central Asia and Russia reverted back to authoritarian regimes (Coleman and Kaposi 2006). Even though Mongolia did not revert back to an authoritarian regime, the corruption index is high, leading to ambiguous evaluations by Transparency International (2020). Mongolians' notion of free expression and independent media, and the media's role in society have been shaped mostly in the online media environment, in which the dynamics of interactions between political elites, the public, and media institutions are radically different from the socialist era.

The collapse of socialism placed Mongolia's untapped natural resources on new emerging markets for global capital. In the last decade, the country's natural resources have lured foreign capital and giant mining multinational corporations, including Rio Tinto and Ivanhoe Mines. Owing to mining development, the country's gross domestic product (GDP) per capita tripled since 1991 (World Bank 2023), and erratic boom and bust cycles have become common. In 2011, the GDP of the country grew by 17 percent, but in 2017 the IMF bailed out the country for 5.5-billion US dollars (Edwards 2017). However, foreign investment inflows into the mines contribute to an economic dependency on extractive mines, leading to an irreversible degradation of the environment and a surge of elite corruption—the situation known as "the resource curse." I explore how the industrial and information society collide and merge in the Mongolian institutional settings by comparing the developments of ICTs and the mining sectors and by analyzing how profits from mining feed back into and shape media spheres.

Along with giant multinational corporations, other Asian investors from China, Korea, and Japan are increasingly tapping into the goods and services markets in Mongolia, especially into the telecommunications and media market. The Korean cultural wave *Hallyu* with its Asian tiger nation reputation, K-pop stars and bands like BTS, and television series have "invaded" the Mongolian culture and influenced beauty aesthetics, consumer tastes, and lifestyle values for years now. Mobile phone services and internet use have drastically increased following the liberalization of the economy thanks to the spillover effect of the Asian microelectronics economies from Korea, Taiwan, and China, and Mongolians increasingly take advantage of this technological availability and geographical proximity.

Influenced by Asian economic growth and with support from funding organizations, the Mongolian Parliament adopted the "Information and Communication Technology Policy in Mongolia" ICT Vision—2010 in 2000 to move forward to build an information society and has been followed up since then in legislation and government services. At the dawn of the twenty-first century, the country lacked the resources necessary to build the pillars of a "knowledge economy": communication networks, government digital services, funding for innovation, and human resources (Johnson et al. 2005). The government policy either did not get much attention from the public or received criticism or even mockery.[1] I document how, over the last three decades, government policy, businesses, and civil society made strides to increase the number of smartphone users and the number of media outlets, and helped to improve government digital services. Thanks to these developments, Mongolians increasingly participate in the digital public spheres, yet are still constrained by economic structures, geopolitics, an uncertain legal environment, and the political context in which the elite increasingly "capture" media. I strive to synthesize these developments of ICT and media in relation to global media governance, not in isolation and not in separate media spheres. Below, I relate varying theoretical perspectives of informational spheres in developing countries to the digital public spheres in Mongolia.

Theoretical Underpinning of Information Society and Media in Mongolia

In this book, I strive to provide an empirical account of the confluence of information society and globalization in Mongolia from the perspectives of information society and media studies. Positioning the developing country of Mongolia on the global information society map is challenging, considering the nomadic culture, sparse population, struggling economy following the collapse of communism, and the recent expansion of extractive mining. These characteristics of Mongolia might not pass muster for the characteristics of the information society that theorists Daniel Bell (1976) and Manual Castells (2000) canonically defined, emphasizing the roles of the service sector in the economy and the pervasiveness of information throughout all spheres of society. Castells (2000) defines the information society as "informational, global and networked" because of its "dependency on generating, processing and applying knowledge-based information" (77).

1 A broadcast show lightly mocked the policy saying that a tiger economy became "a squirrel economy" (*herem uls*), and showed a vignette of everyone eating pinecone nuts, one of the fall scenes in the capital Ulaanbaatar.

The process-oriented characteristics of theoretical information and the networks that instantaneously transmit information are the characteristics of an "information society," in which technologies like the internet and mobile phones are seen as modernizing change agents. In this modernizing approach, a society or a developing country jumps on the bandwagon of adopting new technology in order to catch up over a certain period of time, depending on their resources, wealth, and education levels.

ICT is often at the center of globalization and antiglobalization debates. While no agreed-upon definitions exist for either globalization or information society, many agree that the world's culturally and economically different localities are more interdependent than before, partially due to the free and fast information flow and the internet. Scholars have written about how a new informational mode of development that originated in the United States and other developed countries has spread to East Asia and other developing countries concomitant with globalization. In the 1990s, a new global informational and networked economy emerged all around the world that is qualitatively different from the previous economies in its mode of production as well as in the mode of development. This socioeconomic development is centered around a set of informational technologies, including microelectronics, computers, the internet, and telecommunications (Castells 2000). Many of these technologies were created between the 1950s and 1980s in the United States, but they rapidly spread to the world in the 1990s, coupled with the deregulation policies in the US and other developed countries.

The East Asian countries of Taiwan, Singapore, South Korea, and recently China have rapidly industrialized, partially due to the production of computer and communication equipment and services and by exporting them to the US and other developed countries. Their developments are often exemplified in economic globalization studies, in which free trade, new technology, and foreign investment benefit both developed and developing countries (Stiglitz 1996; Summers and Vinod 1993). These informational economies are characterized by the production of technological products for networked enterprises like Cisco, Amazon, and Microsoft, as well as by complex informational financial services such as stock market derivatives, security software, and online shops. In other words, networked global enterprises started to produce, distribute, and circulate ICT services and products in real time at a global scale utilizing the decentralized networks. However, political economists studying East Asian developing countries highlight the role of institutions and government policies that skillfully bargained with transnational companies in retaining capital, technology, and jobs in their countries. The ideological aspect of globalization, as well as the roles the nation-states play in bargaining with multinational corporations, is often underplayed in the analysis of Southeast Asian industrialization (Amsden 1985; Hveem 2002; Weiss 1997).

The proponents of the globalization thesis tend to emphasize this informational acceleration and the roles media play in disseminating ideas and services in the late twentieth century (Appadurai 1996; Lule 2012). Others argue that "globalization" is a euphemism for neoliberal economic policy, which enables multinational corporations to evade taxes, damage the environment, and stagnate labor wages. In the current era, the forces of neoliberal globalization or "globalization from above" encounter backlash from the left and the right all around the world (Flew 2020). The rise of populism around the world in recent years shows that a significant number of people, mostly bound to their localities, feel "left behind" and they tend to resist global elites (Flew 2020). Contrary to the forecasts of global information society proponents (Castell 2000; Bell 1976), service sector workers have increasingly been subjugated to the impatient or "footloose" capital all around the world (Flew 2018; Garnham 2000).

The trickle-down neoliberal economic policy led by the Bretton Woods institutions—the International Monetary Fund (IMF) and the World Bank (WB)—incentivized foreign direct investment and implemented brutal economic austerity measures in Latin America and Africa in the 1960s and 1970s and post-communist countries in the 1990s. These institutions saw in this networked economy paradigm new possibilities for restructuring the global economy and facilitated its spread to developing countries at an accelerated pace using various incentives such as loans, foreign direct investment, and trade contracts, as well as penalties for not liberalizing or privatizing the markets. When developing countries follow the patterns of consumption of developed nations in an effort to catch up, the only people who benefit are the corporations in the developed countries (Hamelink 2001). This economic adjustment concurred with the collapse of the Soviet bloc and the financial crises in Asia, adding new impetus to the momentum of global capitalist restructuring. The policies of the Bretton Woods institutions, coupled with deregulation policies of the 1990s in developed countries, put an end to the international development paradigm and replaced it with economic liberalization programs with little effort into development. Development efforts of these institutions were mostly operated by aid, donors, and civil society organizations in order to offset the economic and societal consequences of the structural changes in developing countries. These economic austerities often hurt developing countries, affecting their democratic processes, while small-scale development projects run by not-for-profit organizations funded by Western charity organizations do little to mitigate the problems of austerity measures (Young 2001, 55).

Other globalization proponents imagine "globalization-from-below" or "neo-globalization," in which the rule of law is exercised, the entrenched power of the global elite is checked, and international civil society organizations and local institutions play more central roles (Kaldor 2008; Flew 2020). In a broader sense, civil society is defined as a heterogeneous form of organizations, ad hoc associations, and various information and value exchange systems that negotiate contracts and social relations between individuals and political and economic authority (Keane 2003; Kaldor 2008). However, in recent years, the world has seen a decline in global civil society and democratization (Damarad and Yeliseyeu 2018; "Rise of Digital Authoritarianism" 2018), and the solidification of power by transnational corporations and nation-states. Environmental, human rights based, or other interest/affinity groups at the global scale still do not have structures and institutional frameworks to challenge either nation-states or corporate power (Flew 2020).

The inclusion of developing countries like Mongolia into the global information society and the discourse about the inequalities between developed and developing countries was spotlighted during the UN-sponsored World Summit on the Information Society (WSIS) between 1998 and 2005 (Warschauer 2003). During these meetings, the governments of non-Western countries, including China, Russia, and Saudi Arabia, invoked the cultural rights of those who do not have access to technology and do not speak English, and argued for the multilateral governance of the internet and media institutions. However "politicized" this discourse was, international organizations, including the United Nations Educational, Scientific and Cultural Organization (UNESCO) and the Internet Corporation for Assigned Names and Numbers (ICANN), have developed inclusive policies and technological standards to ameliorate technological, linguistic, and economic inequalities in the increasingly globalized world. Otherwise, new technology like the internet in an already unequal society exacerbates existing disparity between developed and developing countries, also known as the global digital divide (James 2013; Norris 2001; Stevenson 2009; Qureshi 2012; Warschauer 2003). The term "digital divide" dichotomizes "haves," who have the knowledge and resources to use information technology, and "have-nots," who do not possess such knowledge and resources. According to this knowledge gap thesis, people with better socioeconomic status, better education, and greater resources tend to adopt earlier and faster than the general public with less education and fewer resources, and the gap increases over time.

The abundance and low entrance threshold of digital media have increased the number of online media outlets, leading to a "hybrid" political media environment in which the ways political information is created and circulated have changed (Chadwick 2017; Voltmer et al. 2021). Political elites in quasidemocracies must accept some plurality of voices in the age of social media, but in praxis, they routinely instrumentalize media for their own political and economic purposes. When newspapers move online, and television stations and cable networks stream all day, they compete for purportedly infinite ads, thus lowering the cost of advertisement in local media. In Mongolia, the small media market and the scarcity of advertising money in local news media interact with the increasing takeover by big digital platforms, exacerbating their economic vulnerability. This situation makes them easy targets to be captured and weaponized by politicians and corporations as media scholar Schiffrin (2021) and others observed in different countries.

New global institutions such as ICANN have emerged centered around the "central organizing pillar" in global media and communication policies (McQuail in Mansell and Raboy 2011, 2), as the power of dominant multinational corporations (MNC) like Google, Amazon, Microsoft, Apple, and Microsoft (GAFAM) has been unbridled in implementing neoliberal economic agendas onto developing countries (Mueller 2010; Stevenson, 2009). Despite various criticisms of these institutions, in this book I argue for the usefulness of the international policies of media governance institutions. Mongolia recently made significant strides in increasing access to mobile phones and the internet and carried out government-led programs toward an information society. In the last decade, social networks such as Twitter, Facebook, and YouTube have become a major source of information for many Mongolians. Like in other countries, Mongolians revere these technology corporations and often overlook their profit-making motives. Most Mongolians believe in the inevitable benefits of technology and have little understanding of their embedded "algorithmic biases" (Woolley and Howard 2016) or the "shadow texts" (Zuboff 2019, 186) of social media.

In media studies globally, researchers apply the theories of deliberative democracy and posit that communicative and informational potentials afforded by the internet and new social media allow people to engage in online deliberation or the "public sphere" (Habermas 1989) by discussing common affairs rationally and freely (Dahlgren 2005; Halpern and Gibbs 2013; Lokot 2020). The internet and social media platforms are often unproblematically associated with increased access to information, thus, robust dialogue and deliberation in emerging democracies. Social media platforms enable connectivity, networking, and dialogical interactions, yet they sometimes constrain certain actions following their inherent "hidden" algorithms of tracking and profiteering (Bucher and Helmond 2017; Poell and van Dijck 2015).

Shoshana Zuboff (2019) in her book *The Age of Surveillance Capitalism: The Fight for Human Future at the Frontier of Power* provides convincing accounts of a new form of surveillance capitalism in which human experiences and private communication activities are inconspicuously dispossessed from people by surveillance capitalists entities like Google, Apple, Microsoft Amazon, and Facebook to create "predictability products" for advertisers and stockholders in addition to natural and capital resources. This new surveillance capitalism radically differs from previous capitalist relations in their relationship with the "masses." They are much more removed from the workers who would have produced and bought their products as in the case of General Motors, for instance, which needs the masses in both producing the cars and purchasing them. Big tech companies employ fewer employees and their products, like a parent vaccination Facebook group or Instagram photo, do not cost a thing for Facebook, for example, and are created by individuals who believe in choice and self-determination in constructing their "self" online. Omnisurveilling corporations that know everything about their users and that also master "accumulation by dispossession" (Harvey 2003) and behavioral instrumentation techniques, constantly track, nudge, and surveil everyone (Zuboff 2019). The surveilled, on the other hand, know little about the corporations and are often full of angst and distrust in our hollowed out institutions.

Following the lines of critical scholars who position the "information society" within broader digital capitalism (Schiller 2000; Hassan 2004) and, lately, "surveillance capitalism" (Zuboff 2019), I intend to contribute evidence from the periphery. This way, the historically prominent "information society" thesis by theorists such Castells (2000) and Bell (1976) in the twentieth century will be contextualized in Mongolia. How do Mongolia's institutions, society, and culture encounter the global information society? How do media that went through radical political and technological changes shape Mongolian society and culture? How is this media shaped as well by Mongolian society and culture? These are the questions I strive to answer in this book. I examine Mongolia's information society and media development in a broader, globalized media context and in relation to international media governance policies and practices.

Historical Origins of Mongolian Communication Systems and Media

Chinggis Khan's empire and its efficient pony express military campaigns and communication system are documented in *The Secret History of the Mongols*, half epic and half historical work written in the thirteenth century by an unknown author, who was close to the inner circle of the Mongolian court ("The Secret History of the Mongols" 2001). The author historically documented the rise of the empire and its military sagas. Even though the text in printed form was lost for a long time, it has played a significant role in Mongolian oral history and in preserving national identity during the colonial period. *The Secret History of the Mongols* is studied in schools in Mongolia following the democratic revolution of 1990, and people often refer to excerpts of the text as unifying passages for the nation. During the socialist era, Chinggis Khan was portrayed in textbooks as a bloodthirsty tyrant and any attempt to reevaluate this position was prohibited by the communist party. He was loathed by the Russians because of the two-century colonization of Russia by the Mongols, but his historical role was reevaluated by the reformers. Mongols now see him as the founder of the Mongolian State.

The independent Mongolian monarchy led by the religious leader Bogd Khan, at the beginning the twentieth century was short-lived, from 1911 to 1919. Mongolia announced its independence from China in 1911, taking advantage of the Chinese Revolution. However, Chinese troops of the nationalistic government of China led by the Kuomintang party invaded Mongolia in 1919, and in 1920 the Russian anti-Bolshevik group called the White Guard entered Mongolia promising to restore the "Yellow Faith Lamaism" (Sanders 1987). In 1921, a small revolutionary group led by Sükhbaatar and Choibalsan with the military support of the Red Army and financial aid from the Comintern (Communist International) in Mongolia established the Mongolian People's Republic. Mongolia became the second socialist country in the world and remained so until the democratic revolution of 1990.

The socialist legacy in Mongolia was characterized by communist party rule under direct guidance from the communist party of the Soviet Union. People's individual freedoms were limited; people were isolated from the outside world, and they suffered from an inefficient, centrally planned economy. The communist party ideology was based on the principles of democratic centralization at all levels of society. Democratic centralization meant a chain of command from the top down, majority rule, unquestionable loyalty to party ideology, strict party discipline, and the superiority of higher party bodies over lower ones (Tumur-Ochir in Sanders 1987). Each economic and social unit in Mongolia had a body of the communist party overseeing its activities. The communist party carefully appointed each government, political, and economic position based on loyalty and ideology. This system of personnel appointment was called the communist party "*nomenklatura* system" (Sparks and Reading 1998, 32). Ideologically, through democratic centralization, the *nomenklatura* system and various secret police institutions, the communist party built a state surveillance system. Socially and culturally, despite the repressive party state, the socialist legacy brought modernization and a social welfare system into Mongolia. Higher education was free, and the social welfare system was universal, yet there existed elite hospitals for high party members and special Russian schools for their children. It is not an easy task to evaluate the socialist legacy in Mongolia. Social welfare achievements of the socialist era are acknowledged even by such anti-Soviet democratic leaders as Baabar (1999). As I further discuss in chapter 2, the foundation of media systems in Mongolia, from the publishing house to radio and television networks, was laid out during the socialist era. Journalists and media practitioners, many of whom are women, gained education and worked as professionals, especially in the later stages of the socialist period. The socialist Mongolian state was repressive, especially during the earlier period. To maintain a regime that was so foreign to many Mongolians who were deeply religious, and tied to their ancestors' history and tradition, the communist party purged counterrevolutionaries, religious recalcitrants, feudal or capitalist elements, and critical intelligentsia. One of the earlier purges of the communist party was against Buddhist monasteries, the main ideological enemy of the communists. Confiscation of monastery property was followed by the demolition of monasteries and banishing of monks. Obviously, the economic policy of collectivization (*negdels*) of the pastoral nomadic economy and the expropriation of feudal properties by the state faced enormous resistance in the 1930s.

The somewhat egalitarian education and social welfare system in Mongolia created educated young people who were open to ideas of *perestroika* and *glasnost* taking place in the mid-1980s Gorbachev era in Russia and Eastern Europe. The Mongolian government led by the communist party was adopting similar policies for economic restructuring (*öörchlön baiguulalt*) and openness and freedom of expression (*olon urgalch uzel*) that paralleled perestroika and glasnost. Reevaluation of history, the relationship with Russia, and the questioning of the legitimacy of communist party rule all took place during these years of openness. However, slow changes and an economic downturn frustrated the raised expectations of people. Young intelligentsia and students wanted more radical changes in the political and social life of Mongolia. The fall of the Berlin Wall in 1989 and the anticommunist revolutions in Eastern Europe favorably influenced the 1990 Democratic Revolution. Kaplonski (2004) and Rossabi (2005) point out the irony that many leaders of the democratic revolution of 1990 were the children of the politburo leaders of the communist party.

During the harsh winter of 1989–90, the Mongolian Democratic Coalition led by young intelligentsia and students organized a series of protests. This coalition demanded the resignation of the government, the establishment of a multiparty political system, and changes to constitution article 82 that legitimized the communist party as the only legal political party. To press the reigning communists, ten reformers went on a hunger strike between March 7 and 9, 1990 on Sükhbaatar Square. This hunger strike was supported throughout the country. The politburo resigned on March 9, and an interim government was established. In July 1990, the first parliamentary election with multiparty participation took place.

Though the 1990 Democratic Revolution occurred without violence, many reformers' lives were at stake. Western scholars have given little attention to the 1990 revolution in Mongolia (Kaplonski 2004; Rossabi 2005). The literature on the revolutions that took place in former socialist countries during 1989–90 argues that these revolutions were largely "melancholic" or "negotiated" (Holmes 1997; Sparks and Reading 1998). However, as Holmes (1997) notes in her book *Post-Communism* the events in these former socialist countries were unquestionably revolutionary in terms of their outcomes and the way they happened. She calls the democratic revolutions between 1989 and 1991 "double-rejective revolutions" (14). That is, they threw off both external domination by the former Soviet Union and the repressive communist party control. Indeed, the democratic revolution, as well as the aftermath developments in Mongolia, showed the rise of nationalism and the rebirth of religion that had been outlawed during the socialist period. Mongolian traditions, Mongol traditional script, and images of Chinggis Khan suppressed during the socialist era were reintroduced by reformers.

Since the democratic revolution of 1990, Mongolia has been transitioning away from the communist political system and a centrally planned economy toward democracy and a market economy. The direct result of the democratic revolution of 1990 was the ratification and adoption of the new Constitution of Mongolia in 1992. According to the new constitution, Mongolia established a mixed, parliamentary/presidential government system with independent legislative, executive, and judicial branches. The legislative branch represents the unicameral State Great Khural with seventy-six seats elected by popular vote to serve four-year terms. The executive branch is headed by the president, elected by popular vote for the period of four years. The president has the power to veto bills, but can be overruled by a two-thirds majority of the parliament. The parliament appoints the prime minister and the cabinet in consultation with the president. The new political system has faced several challenges in the fifteen years since independence that triggered constitutional crises and led to frequent resignations in the government (Ginsburg, 2005).

Postcommunism in economic terms means replacing a centrally planned economy with liberalized economic systems and replacing state and collective ownership of enterprises with private ownership. Liberalization tends to mean a liberal price system that is coordinated by market competition rather than a centrally planned distribution of resources and wealth. In postcommunist countries, massive privatization programs took place using the different methods of a voucher scheme, an employee share scheme, a joint venture with foreign ownership, and direct foreign investment. Radical economic changes have led to the noticeable deterioration of the social welfare system which has become a source of nostalgia for the socialist era.

Media and Mongolian Identity

All sorts of media, from text messages to music, have become a part of who we are, what our identity is, and what we aspire to become. We fuse media into our lives to such a great extent that media construction has become essential to our everyday lives (Deuze 2011). The internet and media coming from outside of the country bring unknown, distant imaginaries and differing values, and tend to undermine national identity (Poster 2001).

Communication scholars Albert Bandura (1986) and George Gerbner et al. (1980) explain how young people learn socially from media and how television shows "cultivate" values in the long term. Media's cultivating effects can be seen by examining the influences of Korean television dramas on Mongolians over the last twenty years. The recent inroads of the Korean cultural wave, from the boy band BTS to a myriad of television dramas on Mongolian television channels, have persistently influenced the value systems and national identity of Mongolians. Korea is the fourth-largest trading partner of Mongolia after China, Russia, and Japan, but the Korean cultural influence on Mongolians has spread widely and persistently. In 2004–5, for example, the television drama *Dae Jang Geum*, about royal chef *Dae Jang Geum*, "taught" about Korean cuisine, history, and business ethos and swept the city streets empty when the show was broadcast on television. Over the years, many Mongolians learned from Korean dramas how to keep a house, wash clothes, or conduct business. Supermarkets like Emart, restaurants like *The Bull,* and convenience store GS25 in Ulaanbaatar all emulate Korean stores and products. Savvy Korean businesses effectively leverage their sales with product placement and advertisements in television shows and other media and then stock the shelves.

The role of media in constructing Mongolian identity is one of the foci of this book. The relationship between the concepts of national identity and nationhood is often fraught. In media studies, the media's role has been double-sided, helping to construct and deconstruct national identities. While the printing press contributed to the formation of nation-states, new digital media contributed to the undermining of nation-states. The printing press and written scripts have factored into the uniformity and standardization of national languages and, thus, of national identity. One might argue that *The Secret History of the Mongols*, a sacred text depicting Chinggis Khan's reign in the thirteenth century could have played a similar role for Mongolians as the Bible did for European nations. Mongol scholars and anthropologists argue that the nomadic aristocracy depicted in the text formed the Mongolian national identity till the twentieth century (Munkh-Erdene 2006; Sneath, 2010). Even many contemporary Mongolians who live in the city identify with their nomadic roots and traditional identity (Empson 2020).

Historically, Mongolians have used a variety of written scripts, of which the longest-lasting script was Uighur of Arabic origin. From the thirteenth century until 1941, the Uighur script was an official written language. However, after the socialist revolution under the influence of the Soviet Union, the Mongolian State in 1941 switched to the Cyrillic alphabet used in the Soviet Union. Some Mongolian researchers argue that the switch to the Cyrillic script helped the government to eradicate illiteracy in the 1940s more than the earlier efforts between 1921 and 1940 using the Uighur script because of the close correspondences of the written and spoken words in Cyrillic (Batchuluun and Khulan 2005). Like other former socialist countries, the literacy program during the socialist era succeeded, reaching 97 percent of the population.

Following the collapse of the Soviet Union, in 1991 the Mongolian Parliament attempted to revert back to the Uighur script from the Cyrillic alphabet; however, this effort was abandoned due to the economic infeasibility. Uighur script is written vertically and has twenty four letters, each letter having three different forms in the beginning, in the middle, and at the end of a word. Since the democratic revolution of 1990, the Uighur script has been taught in schools, but Cyrillic has remained the official written script in Mongolia. The Mongolian state has put further efforts into reviving the traditional Uighur scripts gradually, as documented in the Mongolian Language Law of 2015, which mandates that official state documents and correspondences be conducted in both Cyrillic and Uighur scripts by 2025 (Enkhmaa 2015).

In addition to the Mongolian language, another important construct of modern "Mongolness" is geopolitical. The modern Mongol identity is often articulated as being different from the Chinese and Russians (Kaplonski 2004). The contemptuous distancing from the Chinese and Russian identities has an ironic twist to it, considering Mongolia's economic and trade dependency on its neighbors and the large ethnic Mongol groups living in both countries. Yet, Mongolia has adopted a national, not ethnic, identity construct. Castells (2009) discusses the emergence of the post-Soviet nation-states as an emergence "to assert their suppressed identity" (44). Even though Mongolia was an independent state during the Soviet era, the ideological and economic influences of the Soviet Union were very strong as in other post-socialist countries. As the proverb goes, "familiarity breeds contempt." Historically, after three centuries of colonization by the Qing dynasty (1691–1911), and seventy years of Soviet domination (1921–91), the independent "Outer Mongolian" identity has largely been geopolitically formed. One could say that this identity is built in "in-betweenness" and in contrast to Russian/European and Chinese/Asian identities. Ideologically, during the socialist era, Asian values, customs, and knowledge were associated with being backward and uneducated, while Russian and European education and values were seen as progressive and scientific. During the Soviet era, media mirrored Soviet media and propagandized the population with the superiority of Soviet cultural, social, and technological advancement, and "cultivated" socialist citizens as I will discuss in chapter 2 in detail.

Technologically, the Soviet *Intersputnik* satellite system relayed broadcast radio and television throughout Mongolia. Politically, the radio played the national anthem every morning, while Mongol TV's news programs reached all households with television sets, and helped instill socialist Mongolian identity during the socialist years. I argue that this oscillation between the Soviet past and nostalgia for the Soviet era, on the one hand, and an increasing aspiration for a technologically savvy Asian identity, on the other hand, is a part of contemporary Mongolian identity, at least in the cities.

Toward the end of the Soviet era in the 1980s and 1990s, almost ten thousand Mongolians studied in Russia yearly, and many spoke Russian fluently.[2] Russian authors have described how Russian identity is also split

2 I was one of those students studying in Russia to become an engineer.

between European and Asian identities, where the Asian part of Russia is seen as underdeveloped, and the European part of Russia is acknowledged as more progressive and advanced.[3] During the troubled Sino-Russian period of the socialist era in the 1960s–90s, Mongols allied with the Soviets. The anxiety and guilt also play into the psychic and symbolic inferiority and superiority of "Outer" Mongolians in relation to ethnic Mongols in its two neighbors. Billé (2015), in his book *Sinophobia: Anxiety, Violence and Making of the Mongolian Identity,* argues that the historical Sinophobia of Mongolians toward Chinese is rooted in the internalization of Russian "orientalism." Even though Russia's influence was strong, Mongols held strongly to their ethnic Mongol identities because of the socialist-era restrictions on people's movement, and the marginalized status of Asian ethnic groups like Buryats, Tuvans, and Kalmyks within Russia. It is not surprising, then, that following the democratic revolution of 1990, which overthrew both Soviet domination and the communist party's rules (Holmes, 1997), Mongols turned to nationalism, the Buddhist religion, and the ancestral history of Chinggis Khan's empire that had been suppressed during the socialist period. During the Soviet era, any attempt to reevaluate Chinggis Khan's historical position was prohibited by the communist party, partly because of the occupation of Russia by Mongols in the thirteenth and fourteenth centuries.

On the other hand, language distinction has always been a strong identity marker despite somewhat similar ethnic and racial identities between Mongols and Chinese. The state media cultivated propaganda against the Chinese, including locals of Chinese ethnic origins. The state propaganda was effective because only a few Mongolians spoke Mandarin and understood the Hanzi written system, and Mongols did not intermingle with the Chinese because of the language barriers. This propaganda was also ironically based on othering Inner Mongolians—ethnic Mongolian groups in China—who kept the traditional Mongolian script and ethnic traditions. The Uighur script has remained in use by ethnic Mongolians in China's Inner Mongolia Autonomous Region along with Mandarin Chinese.[4] The patriarchal ideology in socialist Mongolia stigmatized hybridity, ostracized ethnic minorities, and devalued women in social and political spheres. For many Mongolians, the sovereign Mongolian identity meant the exclusion

3 See, for example, Dostoevsky's description of Kalmyks in *Brother Karamazov* and Alexander Kuprin's comparisons of two sisters: Vera, resembling a beautiful Englishwoman, and Anna, a Tatar Mongol princess, in *The Garnet Bracelet.*

4 Around five million ethnic Mongolians live in Inner Mongolia of China as of 2019 according to Chinese Census Data. https://www.stats.gov.cn/english/InternationalTraining/202405/P020201012524513990305.pdf

of hybridity and marginalization of ethnic groups in China and Russia. The nationalistic turn after the collapse of the Soviet system continued othering Inner Mongolians as Chinese, therefore not Mongolians, according to Bulag (1998), who identifies as an Inner Mongolian and researched nationalism and hybridity in Mongolia from 1990 to 1993 after the fall of communism. Bulag (1998) argues that this discourse was the continuation of socialist propaganda that splits national identity from ethnic identity. It appears that this political ideology is still dominating in social and cultural spheres, and Mongols continue to project onto Asians the othering discourse constructed during the socialist era, a process by which Russians themselves sought to demarcate from their "Asianness" as Billé (2015) argues. Here, you see the symbolic impact of texts from the thirteenth century and the socialist state propaganda of the 1970s–80s.

Opening the information and media spheres to the international inflow was one side of the transition from a socialist political state to a democracy. New Mongol identity is also constructed through the dismantling of the state media, which was an ideological mechanism for the socialist state, and by replacing it with new and independent media outlets and cultural organizations. The free agency of Mongolians and their free world citizen identity is even more pronounced on social media platforms. In the last thirty years or more, formerly state-owned media, from communist party newspapers to film studios, publishing houses, radio and television, and telephone and postal services, have mostly been privatized and transferred to public service entities in a short period of time, as I discuss in chapter 2. Ideologically and economically, the liberal media of the 1990s has become an outlet for ostensibly liberated individuals to speak freely and practice agency. Television and broadcasting transitioned to digital television and broadcasting, and the internet and mobile phones have saturated the urban markets and are rapidly flowing to the rural markets. The numbers of media outlets and accessible platforms indicate that people, in general, take advantage of free speech.

However, the institutions' routines and people's perception change gradually and in a continuum, as Caroline Humphrey (2002) explains in her book *The Unmaking of Soviet Life*. Following Humphrey and other postsocialist media scholars (Voltmer 2013; Voltmer et al. 2021), I discuss the "path-dependent" continuity of the institutional routines of the socialist era in modern Mongolia. Opening of the information sphere to international media was a major aspect of the transition from a socialist political state to a democracy. I argue that claiming one's agency and gaining one's voice in open and pluralistic media spheres has become a part of the Mongolian identity projects of post-socialist subjects in the twenty-first century. I examine this part of "unmaking" of the Soviet past and the deconstruction of the socialist identity as a part of the Mongolian identity by examining the concept of "the public interest." I discuss how the term "public interest" gets conflated with the socialist-era term "*нам, олон нийтийн эрх ашиг*" (the interest of the party and the public) that sacrificed the interests of the people in the name of the interests of the communist party. Even after the Law on Public Service Radio and Television was ratified and MNB (Mongolian National Broadcaster) was transferred to public service media in 2005, academic and journalistic circles are not sure which voices the public broadcasters should amplify, or how journalists avoid following the officials in their routines.

The Debates and Arguments about Information Society and Media in Mongolia

Throughout this book, I document how Mongolians, to an unprecedented extent, use ICT and digital media for getting news, learning, entertaining, and participating in politics. Mongolians have joined the global information society by creating Mongolian language content on YouTube and using media to express and participate in their culture and politics using Twitter (now X) and Facebook. The country's relatively young and networked population is responsive to news and information on platforms like Facebook, which accounts for 65–70 percent of online activities, according to Statcounter GlobalStats (2019).

In contemporary Mongolian public spheres, East Asian cultural influences collide with the socialist era's informational and media systems. This book starts with a chapter discussing the production of Mongolian computers Monel and how this initiative was eclipsed by imports of chips and computers from Taiwan, Korea, and China. Datacom's launch of the internet, supported by international aid organizations, also replaced the relatively new informational networks at the statistical office supported by the Soviets. In these processes, Mongolians started to leave behind the socialist identity aligned with the Soviets and move toward a more international and cosmopolitan identity. Unknown to many Mongolians, global governance institutions WSIS, the International Organization for Standardization (ISO), UNESCO, and ICANN have created technological standards and culturally inclusive policies that were helpful in accommodating both Mongolian Cyrillic and traditional scripts on the internet. In this sense, I argue that international organizations fit into the symbolic "third neighbor" Mongolians long for beyond their two powerful neighbors.

Mongolians are eager to express themselves on social media, but they are encumbered by structural deficiencies and the political grip of media by the elite in the context of an unclear legal framework. Contrary to the normative expectations of media, an increase in connectivity and outlets in the digital media environment does not automatically translate into a plurality of viewpoints. A critical and historical examination of the media environment reveals opaque ownership structures, unclear legal frameworks, political capture of media, and financial dependency. As I argue in chapter 2, liberal "yellow" newspapers of the 1990s, new commercial television stations of the 2000s, and online news sites of the 2010s, all struggled to establish themselves with sufficient subscriptions, audiences, and financial independence because of the structural deficiencies of a small media market and limited advertising money along with the uncertain legal environment. In these reoccurring media development cycles, the historical and institutional path dependency of socialist-era media persists, as the media operates on shoestring budgets and only a few media outlets establish themselves financially. The elites exploit the financial dependency of local media, which are competing for a small amount of advertising money and government support, and instrumentalize them for their political and economic goals. The seamless mediatization of politics and culture in relatively open digital media spheres develops at an even pace with the declining trust in media.

The constitution of 1992 promotes a free press and the freedom of speech in the zeitgeist of the 1990s by prioritizing the eradication of socialist-era political censorship and communist party ideational control. When encountering new and unprecedented informational society challenges related to free speech, defamation, and privacy, Mongolian laws fall short in protecting investigative journalists and alternative voices. In 2022, the parliament passed a new batch of laws relating to online media activities, but the "state secrecy clause" unduly burdens journalists in defamation cases and creates chilling effects. Media is frequently instrumentalized by politicians, who exploit the flaws in the implementation process or are protected under the "state secrets" clause and libel laws. Uncertainties in the legal system and new criminalization of false information and defamation excessively burden journalists who investigate politicians and mining deals. Journalistic standards for watching the powerful and exposing corruption are in jeopardy in the current legal system.

In recent years, earlier informational society projects have been directly influenced by big mining projects, extractive endeavors that bring foreign investment along with national debt incomparable to the informational economy. I compare the economic factors of invisible digital capitalism and brute mining capitalism within the debates of foreign investment and debt. I argue that the informational sector experts have created a network of epistemic and knowledge-based communities, which was influential in dealing with multinational companies, whereas the mining experts lacked the epistemic community. Mining influences, as the biggest economic sector in the country, spill over into politics and media, resulting in, for example, an unsustainable number of politically affiliated television stations and favorable media coverage of mining and government contracts. The national public sphere is intensely focused on the contracts between the Mongolian state and the multinational Rio Tinto corporation, and the economy has become lopsided and dependent on mining extraction. Civil society institutions and media organizations push the elite to legislate and develop transparent informational and media laws and practices for citizens; however, the elites manage to create practices that benefit their clientelist policies and these policies constrain media's societal roles and citizen's expressions.

To a limited extent, young reporters and investigative journalists in Mongolia carved out some spaces for their work by taking advantage of the immediate and viral affordances of online and social media, as I discuss of journalism and online websites later in chapter 5. While Facebook's features afford some civic discourse and online deliberation, at the same time the dependency on Facebook as the foremost news source leads to an increase in unsubstantiated, emotionally charged, and sensationalized news as Pickard's (2022) analysis of the American media suggests. For better or worse, news and information on social media challenge the role of legacy media as gatekeepers in Mongolia. At the same time, social media platforms also siphon off advertising money from local legacy media. The promises of "free" platforms and the opaqueness of ownership of the news websites that allow the channeling of political money into Facebook and other online sites need to be critically examined.

Furthermore, politicians and businesspeople sign contracts for nondisclosure agreements with media organizations and conduct pseudopolls without telling how these polls factor into their decision-making. I examine these new forms of political communication by looking into the opinion polls conducted by former Prime Minister Saikhanbileg and current Ulaanbaatar Mayor Sumiyabazar. This veneer of online participation without analysis and policy outcomes does not increase public discussion but tends to simply encourage citizens to vent. *Попрох* or political populism, has become popular in Mongolia as well as in the world, and politicians increasingly utilize new forms of technopopulism in order to garner the support of the public and to legitimize their actions. Populism is common in a liberal democracy and can be compared to the direct democracy approach in the earlier years of the internet. Both the elite and the public have their own dominating and subverting communication strategies that are discussed in chapter 5 in more detail.

Notes on Methodology and Sources

My method and approach in this project combine both social scientific and qualitative humanistic approaches. As a person who was involved in information society projects in Mongolia, and is currently an academic in the communication field in the US, I am interested in globalization, international communication regimes, postcommunism, and development theories that relate Mongolia to the current information society worldwide. Data and excerpts in this book come from primary and secondary sources collected using desk studies, online and in person surveys, and in-depth interviews. During my early career, I studied as an engineer, interned at Monel and managed the internet program of the Open Society Foundation of Mongolia. I include my reflections on significant events, such as the first National ICT Summit in 1999. I also conducted numerous interviews with young people and media professionals over the years, especially during the summers of 2015 and 2019 and a half-year field trip in 2022. The interviews were conducted with flexible schedules in Mongolian, and excerpts were translated into English.

Overviews of the Chapters

The book is organized into seven chapters, including this introduction and a conclusion. The introduction provides the origin and context of media and information society development in Mongolia, and discusses identity projects in the information society as well as major debates and arguments.

In the chapter 1, I trace the historical development of ICT initiatives during the socialist and postcommunist eras. Spotlighted are the first production of personal Monel computers in the late 1980s under the influence of Asian industrialization, the adoption of the internet between 1996 and 97 with the support of international organizations that replaced the socialist cybernetics network, and the ICT Summit and formation of an epistemic community which created ICT Vision in 1999 under the auspices of the UN and the Open Society Institutions. Two cases of Mongolian Cyrillic letter issues in the international standards and the development of country code top-level Latin and international domain names highlight the influences of international media governance organizations.

In the chapter 2, I trace the convergence between traditional media of the socialist era and new liberal media amidst dramatic political and economic changes. The chapter starts with the establishment of the first newspaper and ends with the burgeoning social media platforms used for civic and everyday life. To examine how people's understanding of media concepts such as the public interest and the roles of the press in democracy has been constructed, I examine the transition to digital television in Mongolia between 2014 and 2016 and the rise of commercial televisions in the 2010s. Broadcasting and digital transformation cases show how the elites instrumentalized the media for their political benefits in the blatant way they controlled media during the socialist era and undermined the possibilities for investigative journalism. Media literacy among the public who have lived under the propagandistic media to some extent dovetail with "the hive mentality" or group dynamics of social media.

Chapter 3 examines how foreign investment and new mining wealth influence media and informational spheres in Mongolia. The mining boom in the country from 2008 to 13 tripled the economy, lured an influx of foreign investment, and increased living standards and access to technology for Mongolians. The influence of foreign investment, along with vicious debt cycles are discussed by comparing the mining and the information technology sectors. The mining money cycles back to the public spheres by the increased number of politically aligned television stations and websites, exploiting the unclear legal structures.

Chapter 4 describes the legal environment in relation to the media and informational spheres. Libel and defamation cases in legacy media, misinformation, and commercial speech on social media all test Mongolia's new constitution of 1992. The poor implementation of existing media laws and new provisions on the "state secrecy clause" and defamation cases creates chilling effects for journalists.

In the chapter 5, I provide the cases where new media, gender, and environmental organizations utilize the internet and social media affordances for civic purposes. The civic discourse expands, yet the civil discourse often gets sidetracked or "instrumentalized" by the elite and politicians who also pander to technopopulism.

The concluding chapter summarizes the confluences of media, geopolitics, and platform politics globally and locally in Mongolia. It draws conclusions about what could be learned from the Mongolian case in terms of the media's roles in local politics, culture, and society in the globalized world. It also summarizes how media affect national identity, and the global challenges of social media platforms in local politics.

Work Cited

Amsden, Alice H. 1985. "The State and Taiwan's Economic Development." In *Bringing the State Back In,* edited by Peter Evans, Dietrich Reuschemeyer, and Theda Skocpol, 78–106. Cambridge University Press.

Appadurai, Arjun. 1996. *Modernity At Large: Cultural Dimension of Globalization.* University of Minnesota Press.

Bandura, Albert. 1986. *Social Foundations of Thought and Action: A Social Cognitive Theory.* Prentice-Hall.

Batchuluun, Yembuu and Khulan Munkh-Erdene. 2005. *Literacy Country Study: Mongolia.* UNESCO Report. https://unesdoc.unesco.org/ark:/48223/pf0000146207.

Bell, Daniel. 1976. *The Coming of Post-Industrial Society: A Venture in Social Forecasting.* Basic Books.

Billé, Franck. 2015. *Sinophobia: Anxiety, Violence, and the Making of the Mongolian Identity.* University of Hawai'i Press.

Bucher, Taina and Anne Helmond. 2017. "The Affordances of Social Media Platforms." In *The SAGE Handbook of Social Media,* edited by Jean Burgess, Alice Marwick, and Thomas Poell, 233–53. SAGE.

Bulag, Uradyn E. 1998. *Nationalism and Hybridity in Mongolia.* Clarendon Press.

Castells, Manuel. 2000. *The Rise of The Network Society.* 2nd ed. Blackwell.

———. 2009. *Communication Power.* Oxford University Press.

Chadwick, Andrew. 2017. *The Hybrid Media System: Politics and Power.* 2nd ed. Oxford University Press. https://doi.org/10.1093/oso/9780190696726.001.0001.

Coleman, Stephen and Ildiko Kaposi. 2006. *New Democracies, New Media: What's New? A Study of E-Participation Projects in Third-Wave Democracies.* http://www.ega.ee/handbook/.

Dahlgren, Peter. 2005. "The Internet, Public Sphere, and Political Communication: Dispersion and Deliberation." *Political Communication* 22: 147–62.

Damarad, Volha and Andrei Yeliseyeu. 2018. *Disinformation Resilience in Central and Eastern Europe.* Eurasian States in Transition research center. prismua.org/wp-content/uploads/2018/06/DRI_CEE_2018.pdf.

Deuze, Mark. 2011. Media life. *Media, Culture & Society* 33 (1): 137–48.

Edwards, Terrence. 2017. "IMF Approves $5.5 Billion Bailout Package for Mongolia." Reuters, May 25. https://www.yahoo.com/news/imf-approves-5-5-billion-030728321.html?fr=sycsrp_catchall.

Empson, Rebecca M. 2020. *Subjective Lives and Economic Transformations in Mongolia: Life in the Gap.* UCL Press. https://doi.org/10.14324/111.9781787351462.

Enkhmaa, E. 2015. "Mongolian Language Law is Effective from July 1st." GoGo Mongolia. https://mongolia.gogo.mn/r/146942.

Farber, Jim. 2019. "Steppe Change: How Mongolian Rock Band the Hu World." *The Guardian*, October 22. https://www.theguardian.com/music/2019/oct/22/its-something-new-how-mongolian-rock-band-the-hu-went-viral.

Flew, Terry. 2018. *Understanding Global Media.* 2nd ed. Palgrave.

———. 2020. "Globalization, Neo-Globalization and Post-Globalization: The Challenge of Populism and the Return of the National." *Global Media and Communication* 16 (1): 19–39.

Garnham, Nicholas. 2000. "'Information Society' As Theory or Ideology: A Critical Perspective in Technology, Education and Employment in Information Age." *Information, Communication & Society* 3 (2): 139–52.

Gerbner, George, Larry Gross, Michael Morgan, and Nancy Signorielli. 1980. "The 'Mainstreaming' of America: Violence Profile No. 11." *Journal of Communication* 30 (3): 10–29

Ginsburg, Tom. 2005. "Strengthening Legislative Research and Analysis Capacity of Mongolia's State Great Hural." Unpublished report. The Asia Foundation. Accessed Jan 5 20222 http://www.asiafoundation.org/pdf/Mongoliastrengthening.pdf.

GlobalStats. 2023. "Social Media Stats Mongolia." *Statcounter.* Accessed Jan 5 2023 http://gs.statcounter.com/social-media-stats/all/mongolia.

Habermas, Jürgen. 1989. *The Structural Transformation of the Public Sphere: An Inquiry into a Category of a Bourgeois Society.* Translated by Thomas Burger with the assistance of Frederick Lawrence. MIT Press.

Halpern, Daniel and Jennifer Gibbs. 2013. "Social Media as a Catalyst for Online Deliberation? Exploring the Affordances of Facebook and YouTube for Political Expression. *Computers in Human Behavior* 29 (3): 1159–68.

Hamelink, Cees J. 2000. *The Ethics of Cyberspace.* SAGE.

Harvey, David. 2003. *The New Imperialism.* Oxford University Press.

Hassan, Robert. 2004. *Media, Politics and The Network Society.* Open University Press.

Holmes, Leslie. 1997. *Post-Communism: An Introduction.* Duke University Press.

Humphrey, Caroline. 2002. *The Unmaking of the Soviet Life: Everyday Economies after Socialism.* Cornell University Press.

Hveem, Helge. 2002. "Globalization, Governance and Development: A Political Economy Perspective." *The European Journal of Development Research* 14 (1): 219–43.

Jakubowicz, Karol. 2011. "Public Service Broadcasting: Product (and Victim?) of Public Policy." In *The Handbook of Global Media and Communication*, edited by Robin Mansell and Mark Raboy, 210–29. Blackwell.

James, Jeffrey. 2013. "The Diffusion of IT in the Historical Context of Innovations from Developed Countries." *Social Indicators Research* 111: 175–84.

Johnson, Catherine A., Lkhagvasuren Ariunaa, and Johannes J. Britz. 2005. "Constructing the Pillars of a Knowledge Society: The Challenge of Providing Access to ICTs in Rural Mongolia." *Libri* 55: 216–24.

Kaldor, Mary. 2008. "Democracy and Globalization." In *Global Civil Society 2007/8*, edited by Martin Albrow, Helmut Anheier, Marlies Glasius, Monroe Price, and Mary Kaldor, 34–45. SAGE.

Kaplonski, Chistopher. 2004. *Truth, History and Politics in Mongolia: The Memory of Heroes*. Routledge.

Keane, John. 2003. *Global Civil Society?* Cambridge University Press.

Lhamsuren, Munkh-Erdene. 2006. "The Mongolian Nationality Lexicon: From the Chinggisid Lineage to Mongolian Nationality (From the Seventeenth to the Early Twentieth Century)." *Inner Asia* 8 (1): 51–98.

Lokot, Tetyana. 2020. "Articulating Networked Citizenship on the Russian Internet: A Case for Competing Affordances." *Social Media + Society* 6 (4): 1–12. https://doi.org/10.1177/2056305120984459.

Lule, Jack. 2012. *Globalization and Media: Global Village of Babel.* Rowman and Littlefield.

Mansell, Robin and Marc Raboy. 2011. "Introduction." In *The Handbook of Global Media and Communication*, edited by Robin Mansell and Marc Raboy, 1–21. Blackwell.

Mayhew, Bradley. 2001. *Mongolia.* Lonely Planet Ltd.

Mueller, Milton L. 2010. *Networks and States.* MIT Press.

Munkhbaatar. S. 2020. "E-Mongolia: Mongolia's Digital Transition." https://montsame.mn/mn/read/246236.

Norris, Pippa. 2001. *Digital Divide: Civic Engagement, Information Poverty, and the Internet Worldwide.* Cambridge University Press.

Pavlik, John. 1996. *New Media Technology and the Information Superhighway.* Boston: Allyn and Bacon.

Pickard, Victor. 2022. "Can Journalism Survive in the Age of Platform Monopolies? Confronting Facebook's Negative Externalities." In *Digital Platform Regulation: Global Perspectives on Internet Governance*, edited by Terry Flew and Fiona Martin, 23–41. Palgrave Global Media Policy and Business. Palgrave Macmillan. https://doi.org/10.1007/978-3-030-95220-4_2.

Poell, Thomas and José van Dijck. 2015. "Social Media and Activist Communication." In *The Routledge Companion to Alternative and Community Media*, edited by Chris Atton, 527–37. Routledge.

Poster, Mark. 2001. *What's the Matter with the Internet?* University of Minnesota Press.

Qureshi, Sajda. 2012. "As the Global Digital Divide Narrows, Who Is Being Left Behind?" *Information Technology for Development* 18 (4): 277–80.

Richter, Andrei. 2011. "The Post-Soviet Media and Communication Policy Landscape: The Case of Russia." In *The Handbook of Global Media and Communication Policy*, edited by Robin Mansell and Marc Raboy, 192–209. Blackwell.

"The Rise of Digital Authoritarianism: Fake News, Data Collection, and the Challenge to Democracy." Freedom House, October 31, 2018. https://freedomhouse.org/article/rise-digital-authoritarianism-fake-news-data-collection-and-challenge-democracy.

Rossabi, Morris. 2005. *Modern Mongolia: From Khans to Commissars to Capitalists.* University of California Press.

Sanders, Alan J. K. 1987. *Mongolia: Politics, Economics and Society.* Frances Pinter.

Schiffrin, Anya, ed. 2021. *Media Capture: How Money, Digital Platforms, and Governments Control the News.* Columbia University Press.

Schiller, Daniel. 2000. *Digital Capitalism: Networking the Global Market System.* MIT Press.

Sneath, David. 2010. "Political Mobilization and the Construction of Collective Identity in Mongolia." *Central Asian Survey* 29 (3): 251–67.

Sparks, Colin and Anna Reading. 1998. *Communism, Capitalism and the Mass Media.* SAGE.

Stevenson, Siobhan. 2009. "Digital Divide: A Discursive Move Away from the Real Inequality." *The Information Society* 25: 1–22.

Stiglitz, Joseph. 1996. "Some Lessons from the East Asian Miracle." *World Bank Research Observer* 11 (2): 151–77.

Summers, Lawrence H. and Thomas Vinod. 1993. "Recent Lessons of Development." *World Bank Research Observer* 8 (2): 241–54.

Taylor, Emily. 2016. "The Privatization of Human Rights: Illusions of Consent, Automation and Neutrality." Global Commission on Internet Governance. https://www.cigionline.org/sites/default/files/gcig_no24_web_2.pdf.

"The Secret History of the Mongols: The Life and Times of Chinggis Khan" 2001. Translations by Urgunge Onon, Curzon, 2001.

Transparency International. 2020. "Global Corruption Barometer – Asia" https://www.transparency.org/en/gcb/asia/asia-2020.

Voltmer, Katrin. 2013. *The Media in Transitional Democracies.* Polity.

Voltmer, Katrin, Kjetil Selvik, and Jacob Høigilt. 2021. "Hybrid Media and Hybrid Politics: Contesting Informational Uncertainty in Lebanon and Tunisia." *The International Journal of Press/Politics* 26 (4): 842–60. https://doi.org/10.1177/1940161221999266.

Warschauer, Mark. 2003. *Technology and Social Inclusion*. MIT Press.
Weiss, Linda. 1997. "Globalization and the Myth of the Powerless State." *New Left Review* 225: 3–27.
Woolley, Sam and Philip Howard. 2016. "Political Communication, Computational Propaganda, and Autonomous Agents." *International Journal of Communication* 10 (2016): 4882–90.
World Bank. 2023. The World Bank in Mongolia. https://www.worldbank.org/en/country/mongolia/overview.
Young, Robert J. C. 2001. *Postcolonialism: An Historical Introduction*. Blackwell.
Zuboff, Shoshana. 2019. *The Age of Surveillance Capitalism: The Fight for a Human Future at the New Frontier of Power*. Public Affairs.

1. Information and Communication Technology (ICT) in Mongolia

Abstract: This chapter positions Mongolia on the global information society map and relates its informational quests to the origins of the global information society discussed in the introduction. I describe the history of information society development and the milestones of Mongolian elites' projects that transcend the socialist and postsocialist eras. I argue that, following the collapse of socialism in the midst of telecommunications liberalization and free trade expansion, Mongolians have actively pursued a quest for a new identity that is in tune with the global informational sphere. Soviet-trained Mongol cyberneticists and engineers were influenced by Southeast Asian postindustrial development.

Keywords: Mongolian information society, Mongolian internet, digital nation projects, Mongolian language representation, internet governance

A few Mongolian elite economists and engineers, who were trained in Russia, Germany, Poland, Bulgaria, and Hungary under the auspices of the socialist states' Council for Mutual Economic Assistance (COMECON), were enthused with the idea of technological solutions to the problems of the planned socialist economy in the 1960s–90s. Soviet cybernetics founder Victor Glushkov believed that cybernetics would effectively recuperate the stagnated command economy and would solve "an information processing problem" for Russia (Peters 2016). The cybernetics developments in Russia, on its own terms, was also influenced by American cyberneticists like Norbert Wiener at the RAND Corporation. However, the origin does not determine the end, and the Soviet cybernetics paradigm shifted more toward East Asian electronics development with the production of personal computers by Monel (Mongolian Electronics Co.) in 1986. This prototype of Monel was developed in 1984, when Apple launched its Macintosh computer following Apple I and II. This phase, however, ended abruptly, mostly due to the small

Undrah Baasanjav, *Information Society and Media Development in Modern Mongolia*. Taylor & Francis Group, 2025
DOI: 10.5117/9789463729888_CH01

market of the country and economic challenges during the collapse of the socialist era. My goal here is to contextualize these developments in relation to global economic and political developments.

I will also discuss in this chapter, how the representation of Mongolian Cyrillic and traditional scripts in cyberspace has become a major identity project. Mongolians share most of the Cyrillic alphabet characters, except for the two additional vowels, *Өө* and *Үү*, which do not exist in the Russian Cyrillic alphabet. I will explain the media governance policies surrounding language representation in cyberspace that also intersect with complex technological standards for representing the alphabet characters and the internet's domain names. Unknown to many, over the years various international entities and technical groups have successfully developed media policies, language standards, and technological solutions depicting, rendering, and interpreting the world's languages into digital devices and on the internet (see Baasanjav 2014). The Unicode Consortium, for example, which maintains standards for representing and interpreting modern and historic language scripts, special symbols, and emojis, has played a crucial role in consistently depicting and rendering Mongolian scripts and those two letters. I argue for a connection from this case of representation of the Mongolian scripts to broader language representation and global media policies in cyberspace.

Computer Development During the Socialist State and East-Asian Influences

Mongolia's information technology development first started in efforts to manage the planned economy at Mongolia's National Statistics Office (NSO) in the 1970s following the Soviet cybernetics paradigm that used informational calculations and "feedback adjustments" to fix routine numeric mismatches and mishaps in the socialist planned economy. Soviet cybernetics founder Victor Glushkov once noted that "cybernetics fits our socialist planned economy like a glove" (Peters 2016, 152). In Soviet economic five-year plans, setting prices for commodities and planning factory outputs were done from a center with computational powers. The National Computing Center (NCC) at NSO started to tabulate census data, registration of land resources, and livestock headcounts in the 1970s using the minicomputer Minsk-32 received from Russia in 1974. The new field of computers and cybernetics was dependent on the COMECON's and Soviet's technological and economic support, which also included training of professionals. In the 1980s, the NSO upgraded to ES 1040, a German analog of the American IBM System/360 supercomputer, and started international and domestic exchanges of information with Russia, the Soviet bloc countries, and the Mongolian provinces.

These informational exchanges were precursors to the information society that paralleled the development of the internet in the West. The Soviets were also working on their own informational network such as OGAS (National Automated System for Computation and Information Processing) and ESS (*edinaya sistema svyazi* in Russian), when Paul Baran in the US developed a packet switching protocol at the RAND Corporation and the Defense Advanced Research Projects Agency (DARPA) launched ARPANET (Advanced Research Projects Agency Network) in 1969. Soviet cyberneticists were influenced by American cyberneticists and were working on multiple projects; however, unlike the Americans they faced great resistance from the Soviet military, which refused to open military communication technology and networks for economic and civil purposes. This situation was one of the major reasons for the failure of the Soviet cybernetic projects in comparison to ARPANET, the project that flourished into the internet (Peters 2016).

Training of Mongolian engineers and professionals in information and communication technology at the NSO by a Japanese engineer Kimura *san*[1] was also crucial. Following the establishment of the diplomatic relations between Japan and Mongolia in 1972, Japan's economic support to a new cashmere factory and visits by engineers and scientists to Mongolia started in the 1970s. In 1978, at a microchip calculator repair training, Japanese engineer Kimura *san* got the Mongolian trainees excited about the capacity of small microchips; their compactness and integration levels compared favorably to the mainframe computers Mongolian engineers worked with at the NSO, which weighed tons of kilograms and occupied hundreds of square meters. After that training, NSO engineers G. Oyunbayar and O. Batsukh, along with other engineers from the National Meteorology Center and the Physics Institute led by Dr. Yalalt, started to work on microelectronics projects and created the first microcomputer prototype based on the Intel microprocessor and registered it as the *Och* ("flame" in Mongolian) computer in 1984 (Oyunbayar, n.d.). The compilation of the first computer prototype in 1984 by putting together hard to find computer parts during the socialist era

1 Oyunbayar G., one of the inventors of the first Mongolian computer who worked as an expert for the Open Society of Mongolia, has written a memoir blog, "History of the first Mongolian computer" (Oyunbayar, n.d.). The full name of this engineer is not provided, and the socialist-era records of the visitors from Japan were not recorded.

and making it work with software was important for several technological and sociocultural reasons. This invention opened the door to producing Mongolian personal computers. Starting in 1986, a Mongolian electronics company (Monel) compiled and sold Mongolian-made personal computers and television sets and branded them as Monel. The company was a spin-off led by Dr. Yalalt. At that time, computers were the crux of the information age, and with the start of Monel personal computers Mongolia's cybernetics development started to diverge from Soviet practices.

Most importantly, the start of Monel was a harbinger toward East-looking ICT development. In the early 1990s, Mongolian engineers were mostly trained in the Siberian cities of Novosibirsk and Sverdlovsk, and only a few Mongolian professionals were trained in other COMECON countries. Novosibirsk, within which Siberia's Akademgorodok was located, was known as one of the main places of Soviet technological innovation because of its tie to the Siberian branch of the Russian Academy of Sciences (Castells 2000, 35; Peters 2016). For Castells (2000), these localities were an important part of information society, creating synergies between technological innovations and applications, and bringing together start-up companies and entrepreneurs, comparable to Silicon Valley or Hong Kong. At the end of the 1990s, Siberia's educational institutions were theoretically strong, but technological innovations were economically strapped. Even though personal computers and minicomputers like the PDP-11 were becoming available in Novosibirsk and other Russian cities in the early 1990s, Siberia's institutions and colleges were left far behind compared to East Asian countries in microelectronics and computer productions due to the collapse of the socialist system.

I was one of the students studying computer science in Novosibirsk, Russia, and I also had a chance to intern one summer at Monel, then a small start-up company in the new Cultural Palace in Ulaanbaatar. During my two-month summer internship, I practiced computer-aided design for sketching circuit boards with AutoCAD. During that internship, I first saw Intel microelectronic chips, learned to design with computer software, and even played Pac-Man or Tetris during breaks. This training was much more hands-on and practical than writing computer programs on a mini-PDP or on mainframe machines in Novosibirsk.

At the time, many organizational changes, convergences, and different economic models were happening in Mongolia's transitioning economy. Professionals in the field started to realize how far ahead the East Asian industrialized countries were compared to the Soviet bloc in producing computers and informational devices.

Monel produced thousands of Mongolian computers and television sets in the 1980s and 1990s. Those who worked at Monel had enormous drive and erudition and worked late hours, even overnighted in their offices, as I saw during my internship. They also hoped to step into a new informational age somewhat comparable to other Asian countries by producing personal computers, television sets, and electronic devices. Those young intelligentsia and engineers at that time questioned the principles of the socialist economy and sensed the potential of the looming informational economy. They felt the coming collapse of the socialist economy earlier than the rest of society. Later on, I learned how a few Monel professionals following the regime change became politicians, parliamentarians, and civil society leaders. The Monel office in the center of Ulaanbaatar helped promote the new democratic party in the 1990s, utilizing information technology like computers and photocopying machines, as Burmaa Radnaa, who was an engineer at the company, reminisces in her interviews with Buyandelger (2022).[2]

Understandably, Monel did not succeed in the small market of Mongolia against less-expensive imported computers and communication devices from East Asia. In the 1990s, Mongolia went through a severe economic structural adjustment period into a new market economy following the collapse of the socialist economy. There was no government policy or economic support for creating domestic products and innovations, and new private companies, including MCS and Bodi Co., started to import computers and electronics from Singapore, Taiwan, Hong Kong, and China into the small market of Mongolia. East Asian countries incentivized their exports while protecting their ICT industries with an import substitution policy and this spillover effect was insurmountable for a small start-up like Monel. Had there been a government policy providing loans or government contracts, then the knowledge base or the epistemic community in Mongolia might have developed differently. In other words, the collapsing economy and changing political regime of the 1990s molded the fledgling information economy, pushing a move toward using rather than producing ICT.

East Asia's electronic industrialization and rapid economic growth unquestionably affected Mongolia during and following the years of the collapse of the Soviet bloc. The decreasing price of communication equipment in Asia and increasing liberalization of the telecommunications market in Mongolia allowed Asian companies to tap into the Mongolian market,

2 I remember how Monel engineers sang along with *honhny duu* (the bell sound), which was the anthem of the democratic party. Later, I worked with Burmaa Radnaa when she was a board member of the Mongolian Foundation for Open Society (MFOS).

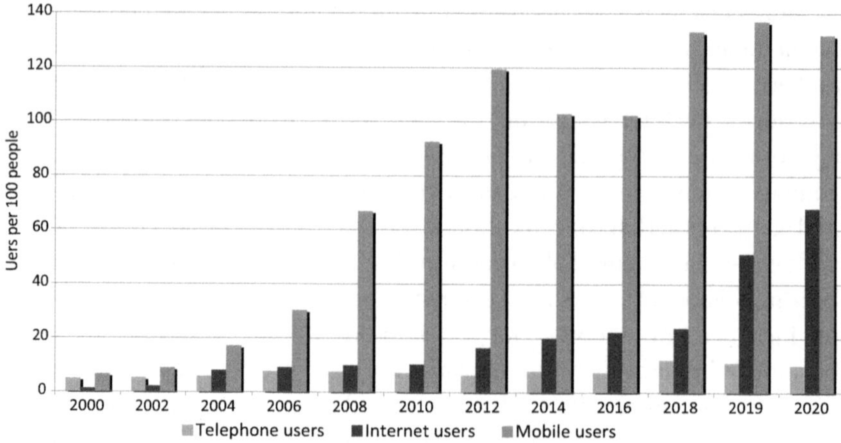

Figure 1.1. The number of users of phones, internet, and mobile phones in Mongolia, 1995–2020. Data is collated from databases of United Nations' Data https://datahub.itu.int/data/?e=MNG and Communications Regulatory Commission of Mongolia https://statistic.crc.gov.mn/.

leading to an increase in the growth of computer and internet use from 1995 to 2020 (see figure 1.1). The number of personal computers exceeded the number of both radio and television sets, reaching 190,000 in 2003 (World FactBook 2005). Despite the low GDP per capita (the Economic Intelligence Unit in 2005 estimated US$477) and the transitioning economy's challenges, this growth in a short time also showed a break from the socialist pattern of consumption that "saved and sacrificed current consumption for the sake of future production" (Krugman 1994).

The biggest producers of telecommunications equipment—China, Korea, and Japan—are among the biggest investors in Mongolia. Japan is the biggest official source of development aid (ODA) for Mongolia, and 50 percent of all Japanese investment in Mongolia goes to the telecommunications sector via companies like Mobicom, a leading mobile phone joint venture company with Japanese Sumitomo and KDDI. Korea Telecom owned 49 percent of Mongolia Telecom Company (MTC) from 1995 to 2018, and the second mobile phone operator, Skytel, is a joint company with Korean SK Telecom. China has been the biggest source of goods and services that make up the shadow or "grey" economy and the second largest importer of goods and services from Mongolia. Communication devices, especially mobile phones, have changed Mongolia's communication drastically in recent years, reaching 100 percent of the population with some people owning two or more phones (See figure 1.1).

The Internet

The first internet node in Mongolia, called the Mongolian Access to Global Information and Communications Network (MAGICNet), was established as a result of the joint efforts of a Mongolian private company, Datacom, with support from the Canadian International Development and Research Centre and the National Science Foundation (NSF) of the United States in 1996 (Corcoran 1996). Mongolian pioneer company Datacom was led by visionary Dr. Dangaasürengiin Enkhbat, who served as the deputy minister of the National Development Council in the early 1990s and as a parliamentarian later. The company was established as a spin-off company from the State Scientific and Technology Committee during the socialist perestroika (restructuring) era. The company was experimenting with new services and financially viable business possibilities with well-trained professionals in digital communications and networking. This private company's launch of the internet with support from the US and Canada established the ethos of an open and unrestricted internet, unlike restricted and controlled communication in Mongolia's two neighbors, China and Russia (Lokot 2020; Morozov 2011).

Datacom established Mongolia's internet connection using Sprint satellite services in January 1996 with two-hundred-thousand US dollars from the so-called "butter fund," which was created by selling tons of butter donated by the US Agriculture Department in 1994. The American Ambassador Donald C. Johnson noted that "Mongolia has a way of communicating with the outside world that does not involve relaying information through its two large neighbors, China and Russia" (Corcoran 1996). Two months later, in March 1996, the NSF helped Datacom obtain a 128-kbps Sprint satellite link from Sylmar, California. Considering the remoteness and vastness of Mongolia's territory, satellites were an appropriate solution compared to the obsolete landline telephone network of the country. The telephone and telegraph infrastructure in Mongolia at that time was outdated and the telecommunications infrastructure was being restructured from a state-owned monopoly to a shareholder company with international investment. In the mid-1990s, international phone calls were prohibitively expensive for data exchange and the Mongolian economy was facing great financial difficulties. Prior to bringing the internet to Mongolia, Datacom provided domestic electronic mail services over the poorly developed telecommunications network of Mongolia. That is why the financial support of international and donor organizations was extremely important for the establishment of internet services in Mongolia. Since then, Datacom has provided email, web services, internet telephony, domain names in both Latin and Cyrillic alphabets, and domestic satellite internet services in some provinces.

The internet in Mongolia was affected by what was happening in the United States. A year before the internet arrived in Mongolia, the US government fully privatized the internet's backbone, NSFNET, which was operated by the NSF. In 1990, the ARPANET project was closed, and a number of spin-off commercial networks that grew out of it came to the cooperative arrangements of private networks in 1995, leaving the internet coordination to the Internet Society, a not-for-profit organization (Castells 2000, 46). The NSF's support of Mongolia's internet in cooperation with Datacom signaled to Mongolians the upcoming freewheeling and privatized nature of the internet. Because the genesis of ARPANET connected American universities, the NSF required that Mongolian universities become connected to the internet. Soon Mongolian universities and academic societies began connecting to the internet. In 1999, a consortium of colleges and universities established their own internet service provider, ErdemNet, which also used direct PC satellite communication for downlinks and provided internet connections to secondary schools. Furthermore, because the internet arrived in Mongolia late following the popularity of the World Wide Web (WWW) in 1993, email and the Web became the most popular internet applications. Many Mongolians were not familiar with other protocols and applications such as discussion forums, CompuServe, or bulletin board systems (BBSs) that fostered big audiences discussing various issues until the recent takeover of online public spheres by social media like Facebook and Twitter.

Mongolians might have missed out on tinkering with earlier applications or even disruptive incidents like the Morris worms that enabled users to practice and experience what Zittrain (2008) calls "generative technology." Generative technology is characterized by openness and accessibility for unanticipated changes by a wide variety of audiences (Zittrain 2008). Nongenerative technology, on the other hand, is sterile and prevents users from adapting, modifying, and creating new uses. Two landmark rulings in the United States, *Hush-A-Phone v. United States* of 1956, allowing a sound muffling device to be attached to a telephone network, and the Carterfone device ruling of 1968, allowing the connection of a radio dispatch device to a telephone network, paved the way for outsider-invented devices to be connected to telephone networks. These rulings set the precedent for enabling radical changes to the telephone networks of AT&T by allowing fax machines and modems. When the privatized internet arrived in the late 1990s in Mongolia, nongenerative technologies like the Microsoft

Windows operating system dominated the market. This trend of privatized and commercialized services has remained strong, while wide audience engagement projects like Wikipedia have not taken off. Mongolians missed out on experiences in creating large-scale projects like Project Gutenberg in Russian, and many have become users mostly rather than producers, as was the case with microcomputers.

The internet is the first electronic media developed in Mongolia after the collapse of the socialist regime. At that time, most enterprises in Mongolia, including the telecommunications operators, were privatized and restructured. They had backward technology and faced many financial difficulties. Globally, telecommunication reforms toward full liberalization and privatization were in full swing in the 1990s. In the 1980s, Great Britain, New Zealand, and the United States all privatized their basic telephone services and were pushing for the opening of state-operated telecommunication markets in other countries, including postcommunist countries. The Agreement on Basic Telecommunications of the World Trade Organizations (WTO), the major international agreement of 1995, mandated that all participating countries open their previously nationalized telecommunications markets to foreign investment and ensure fair competition.

Mongolia's telecom, a state monopoly operator since 1921 with obscure technology and very limited advanced telecommunication services, was restructured in 1995 into a joint venture company with 40 percent of investment coming from Korean Telecom. Mongolia's admittance to the WTO in 1997 further required that the telecommunications providers comply with another major international agreement, the General Agreement on Trade in Services (GATS) of 1997. The WTO agreements mandate that the incumbent supplier of the public telecommunications networks open its access to other competitors on nondiscriminatory and competitive terms and rates. These provisions helped to initiate advanced communications services over the telecommunications network utilizing a variety of technologies including internet services.[3] Mongolia TeleCom entered into the internet service market in 1999 via its subsidiary Micom with better broadband capabilities than the first internet provider Datacom. Furthermore, Mongolia Telecom's network has become important in creating an internet exchange point as well as in increasing network support for other networks such as Erdem, the educational network of universities and schools in the country. Later,

3 "A Need for a New Legal Framework for the Mongolian Telecommunications Sector," Mongolian Telecom Reform National Seminar, August 25, 2000; see also https://www.wto.org/english/news_e/pres97_e/summary.htm

in 2018, the government of Mongolia bought back Korean Telecom's shares in Mongolia's Telecom.

In 1996, when the internet first arrived in Mongolia, there were three other networks in addition to Mongolia Telecom that were run by the state organizations. These networks were operated by the State Meteorological Center, the NSO, and the Railway Authority; all three organizations had outdated technology and faced other difficulties during the transitional economy. That is why Datacom needed to bypass state-operated networks and created a satellite network with American Sprint with support from Canada and the US. Satellite technology has also been appropriate for Mongolia because of the vastness of the territory, the low level of population density, and the underdeveloped infrastructure.

From the very beginning, the internet market in Mongolia was open and privately led, shown by the number of internet service providers (ISP) emerging soon afterward, as well as by the increase in the number of users. As shown in figure 1.1, the percentage of the population using the internet at the end of 2020 reached 68 percent, exceeding the world average and the average percentage of users in Asia, which are 51.4 percent and 44.5 percent respectively (ITU 2021). Until internet services became available over new technologies such as optic cables, digital subscriber lines (DSLs), and mobile phones, the internet access in the country was expensive for most people. ITU and WB (2002) document estimates that in 2002 it cost $35 a month for individual users, while the average monthly salary was $45. That is why, in the earlier years of the internet, almost 70 percent of internet users were businesses, and people used the internet in cafes. Those cafes and internet centers allowed users to pay 1,000–2,000 Mongolian tugriks (MNT) (approximately one–two US dollars) per hour. The United Nations' target price for ICT services is less than 2 percent of the gross national income (GNI) per capita (ITU 2021).

Prices for internet services remained high in Mongolia until mobile phone operators started to provide data packages, especially in the provinces of Mongolia. The unregulated and free advanced communication services policies brought some competition including Mobicom, a joint venture with Japanese Sumitomo, and Skytel, which started as a joint company with South Korean Telecom. Starting around 2007–11, partially owing to the mining boom in Mongolia (discussed in chapter 3), more service providers entered the market including Unitel and G-Mobile. More than half of the population is served by 3G and 4G broadband services (See figure 1.1). The mobile phone operators implemented prepaid card services with SIM (subscriber identification module) and boosted internet use in Mongolia similar to the level of other developing countries. By the end of 2020, the number of mobile subscribers reached 4.22 million more than the population because many people had more than one SIM card.

The relatively open "hands-free" approach in telecommunications services increased access to the internet, but at the same time created a duality in services: better-off urban customers were served with reasonable prices and higher-quality services, while poor groups, especially in the countryside, were left with less access to government services and with expensive rural telecommunication services. This exacerbated a digital divide between the urban and rural residents in Mongolia, the most pronounced digital divide in the country. As the competition in the market ripened and internet access increased, inclusive policies servicing low-income rural communities were needed in order to help these people to participate in the information society.

Information and Communications Technology Policy (ICT)-Vision 2010

Following the examples of East Asian industrialized countries as well as in compliance with the policies of international trade and telecommunications organizations, Mongolian elites have put efforts since the 1990s into developing information and communication technology as a strategic sector. These efforts started with the drafting of the "Information and Communications Technology-Vision 2010", a strategic document meant to push Mongolia's development into an information society. These events happened following the WSIS, and many donor organizations already had programs to bridge the global digital divide.

In 1998–9, a few Mongolian professionals, including former cabinet ministers, and leaders of private companies, supported by the Mongolian Foundation for Open Society (MFOS) and the United Nations Development Programme (UNDP), formulated a blueprint for developing ICT in the country and held the first National ICT Summit (Johnson et al. 2005). The mission of the initiative, as stated in the ICT–Vision 2010 document, was "to promote in Mongolia the development of profound knowledge and intellectual potency, and to improve the quality of life of Mongolians" (UNDP-Mongolia, 1999). This document outlined the objectives of 1) creating a legal and policy framework in relation to ICT development; 2) creating informational and organizational infrastructures; and 3) increasing public awareness of the information society and promoting the value of knowledge among the public beginning in the twenty-first century. The advocacy group members who drafted these documents included the former minister Batjargal Z., MFOS board chairman and internet founder Dangaasürengiin Enkhbat, chairperson of Mongolia's Telecom Company Ganbaatar A., UNDP's ICT officer A. Yamanaka, NGO members Erdenejargal, P., Enkhjargal S., Ariunaa, L., Oyun, R., engineers Altan-Och, G., Odgerel, Oyunbayar, G., Jagdagdorj, E. and the head of the computer science department of the Mongolian University of Science and Technology University A. Erdenebaatar. The drafters of the document also emphasized that the principles of openness, fairness, equality, and universality would be applied in the process of creating a knowledge society in the country. A year later, in June 2000, the Mongolian Parliament adopted the ICT Vision—2010 as a strategic document for further ICT development in the country and issued a resolution mandating suitable implementation plans in the succeeding years (Johnson et al. 2005)

The ICT Vision—2010 acknowledged the emergence of the global informational economy and declared visions, goals, and principles in order to promote a knowledge economy in Mongolia. The process of drafting the document involved a series of roundtables and forums among government organizations, businesses, and research and academic institutions. In this document, the principles of equal opportunity for participation and universal services regardless of geographical location were stated (Altan-Och 1999). Even though the document was aspirational at that time, the process of creating the document was a new, bottom-up way of policymaking by professionals in Mongolia and was broadly discussed among the public.[4]

In the ICT Vision—2010 document, the role of the government is stated to be a major source of information and a driving force for the development of the Mongolian knowledge society. The government of Mongolia, since the adoption of the ICT Vision—2010 in 2000, has regarded information and technology as a strategic growth area, and encouraged investment in the sector. The government has implemented several programs including the Mid-term ICT development (2002–6), Digital Mongolia (2006–12), Broadband Network (2011–5) and E-Government (2012–6) that connected all provinces of Mongolia to fiber optic cables (Munkhbaatar 2020), and started to provide online government services by implementing programs such as the digital citizen card and the government information service kiosk. These efforts toward informational society partially started to work based on the fact

4 At that time, I worked as the internet coordinator of MFOS and managed the funds for programs like the internet for schools, community internet centers in provinces, and training of internet engineers and young users.

that the service sector—telecommunication, transport, trade, and other services—composed one-half of the GDP since 2001 (Chen 2003).

The government of Mongolia has continued its efforts in the development of programs like e-Mongolia despite urgent challenges facing the country and other political hindrances. Yet, the nascent ICT industry itself is small, mostly overlapping with the telecommunications services as of 2015. That is why the government in recent years has set its objectives to provide digital public services for its small population following the example of Estonia, a former socialist country with a successful digital transformation. Estonia, even though it had some ICT sector success, like the invention of Skype that was later bought by Microsoft, focused on digital state services and digital citizens rather than specific electronic or software development (Kattel and Mergel 2019). However, for Mongolia, the legal framework for an information society addressing information security, consumer protection, privacy, digital rights, and universal services has not been adequately developed. At the beginning of the twenty-first century, Mongolian laws did not address universal service obligations or consumer protection and dealt inadequately with cellular and radio frequency licensing and competition. Legal terms such as universal service obligations and public interest debates are detrimental in Mongolia, considering the poverty rate of 30 percent in rural Mongolia (World Bank 2020).

However, the universal service obligations and the public interest definitions have not been reformulated in broadcast and broadband service laws and policies. When businesses skim the "better-off" users and organizations in the capital by providing their ICT services, the "worse off" users and organizations with less economic power, mostly in the rural areas, are left with little protection. Because laws do not define universal service principles and the public interest, the situation leaves no remedy for the poor, often in rural areas, as was the case during the transition to digital television which ended analog television and "dropped worse off" users (Baasanjav 2016). Two relatively new state agencies—the Communication and Information Technology Authority (CITA) and the Communication Regulatory Commission (CRC)—do not have clearly delineated functions in formulating and implementing technology policies and regulations. Furthermore, as I will discuss in chapter 2, the CRC's practices in managing broadcast licenses and setting standards for various multiplatform media were criticized for lack of expertise in television programs and for dependence on the government. If the e-Mongolia program of the government is to be implemented using mobile phone services, the licensing of cellular radio frequencies for fast-approaching 5G technology for the "public interest" needs to be clearly stated in the policy, and the CRC needs to be independent from political whims.

International development assistance and technical expertise were instrumental in addressing the global and societal digital divides in Mongolia. In the late 1990s, the prime minister's cabinet and its ministries established their online presence with support from the UNDP and the Asian Development Bank (ADB). In 1997–8, the Mongolian Parliament first established an internet connection with the support of the Soros Foundation. Furthermore, internet cafes and schools in rural areas, where communication costs and the poverty rate were high, were connected to the internet with the support of international organizations. This support bridged the gaps between the capital city and the provinces and between the organizations with greater and lesser economic resources. In the section below, I discuss how international standards and country code domain names by international organizations helped Mongolian presence and identity in cyberspace.

Mongolian Language Identity in Cyberspace, and Technical Standards

Out of Mongolia's 3.4 million population, 68 percent is online. This is partially owing to various linguistically inclusive policies and technological standards of international organizations. Even though many Mongolians speak English, the lingua franca of the internet, the Mongolian language has been the major marker of Mongolian identity. Academicians and policymakers in the West make arguments for "the linguistic divide" between those who speak English and those who do not because of the "symbolic power" of English (Hobsbawm 1996). This discourse of inequalities was spotlighted, pointing toward the unequal benefits of using the internet, through the UN-sponsored WSIS policies between 1998 and 2005 (Warschauer 2003), and resulted in UNESCO's (2003) *Recommendation Concerning the Promotion and Use of Multilingualism and Universal Access to Cyberspace*. UNESCO's recommendation asks its members to contribute to achieving its goals of increasing multilingualism and universal access in cyberspace and ensuring the participation of the "information poor" in the global knowledge society (UNESCO 2015). This recommendation contains a provision for the promotion of multilingualism in cyberspace, including domain name systems, which led to many controversies in internet governance.

Following the United Nations' WSIS and UNESCO's recommendations on multilingualism on the internet, the internet community has undertaken the unprecedented challenge of incorporating world languages in cyberspace, especially into the root structure of the internet. Multilingualism in the current international law is the subject of "soft laws," not a binding covenant and mostly carried through the directives and recommendations of UNESCO. The inclusion of traditional Mongolian and Cyrillic alphabets into computers and the internet was paramount for Mongolians. Mongolians have clearly faced "the linguistic divide" of the global information society in addition to the infrastructural and connectivity divides.

Internationalization and standardization of the world's languages in computers, software, and internet, including Unicode and Punycode, have been achieved over the years by concerted efforts of various international standard-setting organizations and technology companies. Unicode standards are international standards for interchange, processing, and display of multilingual character sets and diverse written languages by providing "a repertoire of code points used in different scripts, including various classifications of character properties, and normalization rules" (ICANN 2012). Unicode standards allow different languages, including ancient and endangered languages, to be represented digitally. When a user types, for example, a traditional Mongolian letter ᠠ, a browser renders the Unicode code point of (U+1820) regardless of the differences in platforms, software, and language employing the Unicode standard. The latest Unicode 13.0 version has around 143,859 characters representing around 154 languages and 55 emojis (Unicode 13.0).

Even though the Cyrillic script was incorporated in Unicode 1.0 since 1991, two additional vowels, *Өө* (a barred *O*, Unicode points U+04E8 and U+04E9), and *Үү* (a straight *Y*, Unicode points U+04AE and U+04AF) challenged Mongolians in the 1990s due to inconsistent representation of the two letters. Because of this issue, Mongolian language library resources could not be properly indexed, and online activities like chatting were cumbersome. The problem was resolved when Microsoft released a Windows system incorporating the Unicode standard 6.2 in 2007. The traditional Mongolian script used in Inner Mongolia was included in Unicode version 3.0 standards in 1999. The Mongolian state is also planning to adopt the traditional script. The inclusion has been achieved by the collaboration of scientific and technical groups in China and Mongolia within the international standard-setting organizations.[5] This successful collaboration of technical groups in solving

5 See the Unicode consortium's lists relevant to Mongolian script-related documents at https://unicode.org/L2/topical/mongolian/.

the Mongolian language and identity issues outside of the state governments shows the effectiveness of international organizations.

During the United Nations' WSIS meetings, the domain names system, the system of managing textual names of web resources on the internet, became the center of controversies among the nations partially because nation-states like China and Russia questioned the US control of the domain name system (DNS) (DeNardis and Raymond 2013). The DNS converts web addresses written in alphabets into numerical IP addresses. Because of the pure technical nature of the system, it used to be an obscure technical issue until it was brought up by these states. They consist of top-level domain names placed at the very end and sub-domain names separated by dots, and are divided into generic top-level domains (gTLD) such as .com, .edu, .gov, .mil, .net, .org, and country code top-level domain (ccTLD) names assigned to certain countries and territories such as .cn (China), .ru (Russia), and .mn (Mongolia). The internet's root file, a single and globally consistent list of top-level domain names did not recognize Unicode characters and worked only in the LDH (Letters, Digit, Hyphen—as used in the Roman character set) characters (Froomkin 2011; Mueller 2010). A standard called Internationalizing Domain Names in Applications (IDNA) was developed, which converts Unicode character sets (U-label) to a Punycode string in LDH character sets (A-label) prefixed by 'xn' to address this hierarchical nature of the DNS. For example, the Cyrillic name of Mongolia's IDN ccTLD .мон is represented in the string (xn--l1acc). The IDNA protocol specifies rules for determining whether a code point can be included in a domain name and addresses how visually identical domain names known as variants should be managed (ICANN 2012, 10).

The proponents of ccTLDs and international domain names argue that international domain names consisting entirely of native character sets tend to benefit local companies and people who only speak their local languages, and improve access to the internet. This effort has been a step to increase participation by non-Western developing countries in internet governance, which has historically been marginal. In these debates, ccTLDs have become a presumed panacea for language diversity in cyberspace. Mongolia's two big neighbor states—China and Russia—have played vital roles in ICANN's initiation of the internationalization of domain names and have taken full control over the registration of their country code domains (Baasanjav 2014). Scholars pointed out that these states "politicized" the control of the internet by the United States and challenged the US-centric and private-led governance of critical internet resources (DeNardis and Raymond 2013). The DNS root zone file was controlled by the US Department of Commerce, and the DNS's root zone was housed by Verisign until ICANN's transition to a truly independent organization in October of 2016 (Froomkin 2011). However remote these debates are to Mongolians, these debates helped to set the standards that are inclusive of the various linguistic standards.

The domain name system is an important part of global internet governance, and ICANN, the governing body of the internet, manages and maintains them. ICANN is an unprecedented global and multilateral governance regime involving governments, private organizations, civil society institutions, and heterogeneous network actors around the globe. Since its beginning, ICANN has entered into an uneasy relationship with the state-centered international regime. On one hand, as an international governing organization of the internet, ICANN follows the principles of international law, including the United Nations' Universal Declaration of Human Rights (UDHR) and World Intellectual Property Organization (WIPO) treaties (Síthigh 2010) and manages international power relations among the states. On the other hand, as a quasicorporate structure regulating a market worth billions of dollars mostly concentrated in the US, ICANN's authority to represent the public interest of the global internet community has been questioned by non-US governments and international civil society organizations.

In 2009, ICANN approved a new standard for fully internationalized country code domain names (IDN ccTLD) in different scripts other than the Roman alphabet, and since then ICANN has been approving and delegating IDN ccTLDs to local domain name registries and registrars through its fast-track process. Over the years, internet communities grappled and succeeded with the technical challenges of incorporating international scripts into the naming system of the internet by developing the root zone standards and security measures against domain name "spoofing." IDNs make it easier for criminals to impersonate or "spoof" websites by mixing different scripts leading to homograph attacks, phishing, and redirects in order to steal money, information, or goods. The citibank.com web site can be impersonated by replacing the Roman letter c (Unicode character U+0107) with the Cyrillic letter c (Unicode character U+0301), thus luring bank customers to a false site. The two letters look alike and are homographs, and redirecting with malicious intent is called a homograph attack. Cyrillic shares many visually similar glyphs with the Roman, Greek, and the Perso-Arabic alphabets, invoking security concerns surrounding spoofing, impersonation, and homograph attacks. That is why ICANN strongly cautions against mixed characters and confusable collisions due to visual similarities in IDNs. The complexity of technical standards along with language-related standards obscures the understanding and awareness of the security issues in relation to IDN.

While American companies use mostly gTLDs, less developed countries like Mongolia tend to use ccTLDs almost three times more than gTLDs. Mongolian organizations seem to prefer domain names within .mn partly due to the ease of working with the local domain name registrar and partly due to the perceived legitimacy of the nation-state. Yet, domain names in Mongolian are frequently written in English words and acronyms. In 2006, 74.5 percent of the sample of Mongolian websites used English words or acronyms in their textual URL addresses (Baasanjav 2012). In other words, textual web addresses are easier to discern by an audience with knowledge of the English language, even though most internet users rely on search engines to find websites (ICANN 2012). The Mongolian Cyrillic script country code top-level domain name .мон was delegated by ICANN to the Datacom Company, the only private domain name registrar of the .mn suffix. The initiation of IDN ccTLds consisting entirely of native character sets might increase business opportunities for local businesses because they expand the naming systems for non-English speakers.

Conclusion

The chapter discussed how information society has reached Mongolia, and despite the geographical remoteness, the country's computer development, internet adoption, government policy, and linguistic participation have immensely been affected by what happens in other countries, as well as by the policies of international organizations. In other words, the international communication governance regime and civil society, which Mongolians refer to as "the third neighbor," have influenced media spheres and national identity. I showed how the first computer development and government policy in Mongolia since the Soviet era was influenced by Southeast Asian technology and industrialization policy and how internet adoption was closely supported by Canadian and American technology and financial support. Mobile phone use in Mongolia follows the Asian industrialization trend in that social media is dramatically changing the information society, and this will be discussed in the next chapter. I also discussed how much progress the internet community has made in internationalizing cyberspace despite the fact that some goals might have been "politicized" by nation-states. I showed how complex language systems and written scripts have been incorporated into global information society and how these efforts were better facilitated by international organizations than by nation-states. The initiation of non-Western alphabet domain names and the creation of culturally inclusive non-Western script standards have been important steps in achieving linguistic diversity on the internet. These processes involve deliberate efforts by international organizations, technical groups, and multilateral bodies; otherwise, small developing countries and people with diverse cultural heritages would have been further excluded.

Nation-states, for political interests, challenged the global media governance institutions, which have complex inner workings, including task forces and engineering groups dealing with complex technological standards. International standards-setting organizations and internet communities have been successful in solving multilingualism and its technical issues while leaving political aspects to nation-states and state-centered international regimes. Mongolia's case shows how immensely interrelated the global information society is due to accelerated technology and policy at the global level.

Work Cited

Altan-Och, Genden. "Information and Communication Technology Development in Mongolia and Vision for the Further Development." Keynote Presentation at the National ICT Summit, June 1999.

Baasanjav, Undrah B. 2014. "Linguistic Diversity on the Internet: Arabic, Chinese and Cyrillic Script Top-Level Domain Names." *Telecommunications Policy* 38 (11): 961–9.

———. 2012. "Global Digital Divide: Language Gap and Post-Communism in Mongolia." In *E-Governance and Civic Engagement: Factors and Determinants of E-democracy,* edited by Aroon Manoharan & Mark Holzer, 210-234, IGI Global.

———. 2016. "The Public Interest and Transition to Digital Television in Mongolia." *International Journal of Digital Television* 7 (1): 7–22.

Buyandelger, Manduhai. 2022. *A Thousand Steps to Parliament: Constructing Electable Women in Mongolia.* The University of Chicago Press.

Castells, Manuel. 2000. *The Rise of the Network Society.* 2nd ed. Blackwell.

Chen, Kevin C. 2003. "Growth and Recovery in Mongolia During Transition." IMF Working Paper. https://www.imf.org/external/pubs/ft/wp/2003/wp03217.pdf.

Corcoran, Elizabeth. 1996. "How the Butter Fund Spread the Internet to Mongolia." *The Washington Post,* February 29. https://www.washingtonpost.com/archive/politics/1996/03/01/how-the-butter-fund-spread-the-internet-to-mongolia/94d75e36-0680-444a-8929-966af4dfoecc/.

DeNardis, Laura and Mark Raymond. 2013. "Thinking Clearly About Multi-stakeholder Internet Governance." Paper presented at the 8th Annual GigaNet Symposium, Bali, Indonesia. https://papers.ssrn.com/sol3/papers.cfm?abstract_id=2354377

Froomkin, A. Michael. 2011. "Almost Free: An Analysis of ICANN's 'Affirmation of Commitments.'" *Journal on Telecommunications and High Technology Law* 9: 187–233.

ICANN. 2012. *A Study of Issues Related to the Management of IDN variant TLDs (Integrated Issues Report)*. http://www.icann.org/en/resources/idn/idn-vip-integrated-issues-final-clean-20feb12-en.pdf.

ITU. 2021. *Digital Trends in Asia and the Pacific in 2021*. https://www.itu.int/en/myitu/Publications/2021/03/08/09/13/Digital-Trends-in-Asia-Pacific-2021.

Johnson, Catherine A., Lkhagvasuren Ariunaa, and Johannes J. Britz. 2005. "Constructing the Pillars of a Knowledge Society: The Challenge of Providing Access to ICTs in Rural Mongolia." *Libri* 55 (4): 216–24.

Kattel, Rainer and Ines Mergel. 2019. "Estonia's Digital Transformation: Mission Mystique and the Hiding Hand." In *Great Policy Successes*, edited by Malory Compton and Paul 't Hart, 143–60. Oxford University Press.

Krugman, Paul. 1994. "The Myth of Asia's Miracle." *Foreign Affairs* 73 (6): 63–78.

Lokot, Tetyana. 2020. "Articulating Networked Citizenship on the Russian Internet: A Case for Competing Affordances." *Social Media + Society* 6 (4): 1–12. https://doi.org/10.1177/2056305120984459.

Morozov, Evgeny. 2011. *The Net Delusion. How Not to Liberate the World*. Penguin.

Mueller, Milton L. 2010. *Networks and States*. MIT Press.

Munkhbaatar, S. 2020. "E-Mongolia: Mongolia's Digital Transition." Montsame, Dec 14. https://montsame.mn/mn/read/246236.

Oyunbayar, G. n.d. "Монголын анхны компьютер бүтсэн түүх" [The history of the first Mongolian computer]. https://gogo.mn/r/169931.

Peters, Benjamin. 2016. *How Not to Network a Nation: The Uneasy History of the Soviet Internet*. MIT Press.

Mac Síthigh, Daithí. 2010. "More Than Words: The Introduction of Internationalised Domain Names and the Reform of Generic Top-Level Domains at ICANN." *International Journal of Law and Information Technology* 18 (3): 274–300.

UNDP-Mongolia. 1999. *ICT National Summit Report*. Accessed April 15, 2002 from www.un-mongolia.mn.

UNESCO. 2015. "A Decade of Promoting Multilingualism in Cyberspace." http://unesdoc.unesco.org/images/0023/002327/232743e.pdf.

"Unicode 13.0.0." 2020. Unicode, March 10. http://www.unicode.org/versions/Unicode13.0.0/.

Warschauer, Mark. 2003. *Technology and Social Inclusion*. MIT Press.

"Mongolia Poverty Update." World Bank, Mar 6, 2020.https://www.worldbank.org/en/country/mongolia/publication/mongolia-poverty-update.

World FactBook. 2005. Mongolia. https://www.cia.gov/the-world-factbook/countries/mongolia/.

Zittrain, Jonathan. 2008. *The Future of the Internet and How to Stop It.* New Haven, MA: Yale University Press.

2. Media Development: From Socialist to Social Media

Abstract: This chapter discusses media development from the start of the first newspaper to the proliferation of social media platforms in contemporary Mongolia. A pluralistic media environment has been established, starting with liberal "yellow" newspapers of the 1990s and eventually including new commercial television stations of the 2000s and online news sites of the 2010s. Yet, all struggled to establish sufficient subscriptions, audiences, and financial independence because of the structural deficiencies of a small media market. In this emerging media market, the concepts of fair competition, financial independence, media regulation, and the public interest are evolving. The historical accounts help to explain the residuals of socialist-era routines and mentalities in media spheres.

Keywords: Mongolian newspapers, commercial television, media convergence, financial dependency, and the public interest

Media development during the seventy years of the communist era in Mongolia has left its "path dependency" or continuity along the historically developed paths in media routines as Voltmer (2013) and other scholars who studied media in former socialist countries point out (Coleman and Kaposi 2006; Jakubowicz 2011; Sparks and Reading 1998).

Under socialism, state broadcast news *Tsagiin Hurd* reached almost all households, and the workers attended mandatory "newspaper colloquia" (*өглөөний сонсгол*) every morning. This way, media fostered "socialist citizens" with presumed culturally uplifting news and programs. Media content was often "sanitized" from critical views of the party and state, and the communist party oversaw the economy and society with the principles of democratic centralization, loyalty to the party, and the *nomenklatura* personnel appointment system (Sparks and Reading 1998). There was

Undrah Baasanjav, *Information Society and Media Development in Modern Mongolia*.
Taylor & Francis Group, 2025
DOI: 10.5117/9789463729888_CH02

limited criticism of the society in the form of light satirical magazines like *Tonshuul* (Woodpecker) and a few television programs and shows targeting bureaucrats and incompetent workers; however, in a broader sense, critical and subversive texts were highly censored, and their creators were ostracized.

In private spheres, people made sense of their lives through folk metaphors to lighten up the everyday commodity scarcity and subvert the socialist ideology. Anthropologists and historians who study Soviet life discuss how ordinary people infused widely understood religious and political metaphors into rumors to create alternate discourse during Stalin's brutal Bolshevik collectivization (Viola in Coast and Fox 2015). Popular saying describing the low pay of a socialist planned economy, like "they pretend they pay, and we pretend we work," circulated in private spheres. Mongolians embraced "rumors" as a way of challenging elite politics and creating alternate political discourse during the socialist era. The use of rumors as an alternate discourse continues in the sensemaking of politics among contemporary Mongolians, as Empson (2020) observed based on her interviews with her interlocutors. This populistic discourse is ever prevalent on social media. The socialist era path dependency still manifests in self-censorship of media and politicians' instrumentalization of media. Provided in this chapter are historical accounts helpful in understanding the current practices in media outlets over the last thirty years.

Then, the chapter explores how digital platforms and social media proliferated, especially in the capital city Ulaanbaatar. The era of "yellow newspapers" in the 1990s, the emergence of commercial television in the 2000s, and the convergence of traditional media with social media in the 2010s, all unquestionably created informational spheres with a variety of media outlets. I elaborate upon attendant media technology and legal issues and argue that the multiplicity of outlets does not necessarily translate into an increased plurality of voices. The arguments I make are based on the numerical rise of politically affiliated commercial television stations and the transition of state television to public service broadcasting in the country's small media market. A small carved-out space for investigative journalism on digital media, exemplified by journalists Lkhagva Erdene and Budragchaa Serdamba, is increasingly being narrowed by politicians, who use defamation lawsuits against journalists and control the criminal system which poorly implements or skews the laws. Laws do not clearly delineate commercial and political interests from public interests, limiting the media's roles in checking political power.

Early Newspapers

The first newspaper in the country, *Shine Toli* (New Mirror), was launched in 1913 by Tseveen Jamsrano, a professor at Saint Petersburg University who settled in Khüree (Baabar 1999; Sneath 2010), then the capital of the independent monarchy later renamed Ulaanbaatar. The first media was established during the short-lived religious monarchy led by Bogd Khan and reflected the political turmoil of the historical era. In 1911, taking advantage of the Chinese Revolution, Mongolia announced its independence from the Chinese Qing dynasty, which colonized the country for three centuries. The independent monarchy did some modernization, establishing the first printing house, a telephone committee, and a power station. The creation of the newspaper was one of the outcomes of a pact the Mongolian monarchy entered into with the Russian Empire in 1913, in which the Russian Empire and the Mongolian monarchy agreed upon trade between the two countries including mining, fishing, cattle trading, and postal shipments.[1] But, this newspaper did not continue long and published around twenty issues in a magazine format. Damdin Sükhbaatar, the founder of the Mongolian People's Party, worked as a typesetter in the first publishing house, which also influenced him to start the next newspaper, *Mongoliin Ünen* (Mongolian Truth).

Mongoliin Ünen was a partisan newspaper with communist ideology. In the 1920s, political turmoil in China and Russia spilled into Mongolia; the nationalistic government of China led by the Kuomintang party and a Russian anti-Bolshevik group called the White Guards both invaded Mongolia in turns. During this political turmoil, the pro-Bolshevik revolutionary group of Mongolia started to publish a newspaper in Irkutsk, Russia, which carried the propaganda of Marxism-Leninism and the Great October Socialist Revolution" (Sanders 1987, 12). In 1921, this group led by Sükhbaatar and Choibalsan, with the military support of the Red Army and financial aid from the Comintern (Communist International) established the Mongolian People's Republic. Mongolia became the second socialist country and remained so until the democratic revolution of 1990.

Started by the newspaper *Mongoliin Ünen*, state socialist media was a mass mobilization tool and an essential part of the indoctrination of communist ideology. *Ünen* was the central government and communist party newspaper, and within its 102 years of existence it published more

1 Признание автономии Внешней Монголии. [Recognition of Autonomy of Outer Mongolia.] https://istmat.org/node/27315.

than 24,500 issues. During the socialist era, it reached each party unit in the country thanks to the compulsory morning "newspaper reading hours" (*өглөөний сонсгол*) or colloquia. There were no competing or alternative newspapers; instead, *Ünen* had sister newspapers for younger generations titled *Zaluuchuudiin Ünen* (Youth Truth) and *Pioneeriin Ünen* (Pioneers' Truth) and other affiliate labor and literary newspapers supporting the party and government. *Ünen* was the major newspaper of the communist party. The communist party operated on the principle of democratic centralization, and each party unit had a "morning newspaper colloquium" where the party policy was discussed by workplace groups. The current editor in chief Tsoojchuluuntsetseg of *Ünen* says:

> Even though the newspaper was ideological and partisan, its archive over the years has carried the Mongolian history in print and each issue was written and edited by historical figures and intellectual writers like Buyannemekh, Sukhbaatar, Bodoo, Dogsom, Danzan and Natsagdorj. (interview with Tsoojchuluuntsetseg, May 29, 2022)

The newspaper has become a weekly newspaper of the People's Party as of January 2022. I will discuss the newspaper's survival after the democratic revolution of 1990 and its adaptation to a market economy in the next section when I discuss the market aspects of media and economic transition. State ownership and a centrally planned economy suppressed independent and commercial media and media professionals and institutions were trained to self-censor other ideological views and different expressions of cultural representations.

State Radio and Television

The only nationwide radio in the country during the socialist era was Mongol Radio, which started its broadcast in 1931. Mongolian television started to air for the first time in 1967 and broadcast nationally using Soviet *Intersputnik* satellite relay in 1971.[2] In the 1980s, Mongolian television was produced and broadcast in color. Till 1992, the National Agency for Radio and Television made ideological and programmatic decisions in accordance with the communist party policy (Unursaikhan 2019) and

2 https://intersputnik.online/view/ms-bolor-erdene-i-would-say-that-satellites-could-play-an-important-role-to-increase-digital-connectivity-and-reducing-the-digital-divide-in-mongolia-

the cultural mandate to foster "socialist citizens." Mongol Radio started and ended each day with the national anthem and Mongolian National Television's (MNT) news program once reached almost 100 percent of the nationwide audience. Mongolian television and radio were heavily reliant on the Soviet Union economically and technologically and broadcast news and programs closely resembled the Soviets' news and programs because many professionals were trained in Russian universities. *Telekino* studio was the first film studio at the Mongolian National Television, and in the sections below, I will discuss how this studio became a springboard for broadcast professionals to move to the first commercial studios and television stations in 1991.

In over thirty years of broadcasting, MNT built structural and professional teams capable of producing a variety of educational programs, history programs, and programs targeting rural populations and ethnic minorities. When Mongolian television transitioned to a public service entity, Mongolian National Broadcaster (MNB), it inherited from its socialist-era predecessor a long-standing history, a nationwide infrastructure, and trained personnel. This history gave advantages to MNB in competition with commercial television stations that struggled to create Mongolian language programs. MNB's news program *Tsagiin Khurd* had the highest number of viewers in the 1990s, and MNB, for the longest time, enjoyed name recognition and channel loyalty among the population above thirty-five years of age even after many commercial television stations flourished (Maxima Consulting 2014).

Under socialism, there was no commercial media outlet, and information was tightly controlled in all political, social and economic spheres of society. Socialist media discouraged criticism of the economic and political systems. People's individual freedom and judgment were controlled; people were isolated from the outside world, and they suffered from an inefficient centrally planned economy. Through democratic centralization, the *nomenklatura* system (Sparks and Reading 1998), and various secret police institutions, the communist party tightly controlled society (Kaplonski 2004). Media professionals and institutions were trained to censor and self-censor critical information about party leaders and communist ideology.

Even though the ideological control of the socialist state was tight, literary and creative media endeavors emerged during the socialist era. Media professionals, journalists, editors, engineers, and directors created news, films, and television programs for Mongolian National Television. Many of these professionals were women carrying the first Nikon cameras and producing television shows from the countryside for black and white television sets

(Buyandelger 2022). Radio telenovelas, literary and translated work, over the air radio, and television reached almost all homes in the capital and many in the countryside.

Democratic Revolution and The New Constitution

The 1990 Democratic Revolution in Mongolia occurred without violence, much like other revolutions that took place in former socialist countries during 1989–90. Even though the events in former socialist countries were seen as largely "melancholic" or "negotiated" as Holmes (1997) argues in her book *Post-Communism,* they were "double-rejective revolutions" (14) throwing off both external domination of the former Soviet Union and the repressive communist party control. Most former communist countries saw the rise of nationalism and the reintroduction of religion to fill the ideological vacuum left after the collapse of communism. Indoctrination of socialist values meant praising the Soviets while suppressing Mongolian traditions, traditional script, and images of Chinggis Khan. All suppressed national identity symbols and traditions that were percolating under socialism returned strong following the democratic revolution of 1990.

Mongolia's new constitution of 1992 acknowledges the rule of law, civil liberty, freedom of speech and press, and it introduced private property and land ownership. In the constitution, Mongolia established a mixed, parliamentary/presidential government system with independent legislative, executive, and judicial branches. The state censorship authority was dismantled after the passing of the 1998 Law on Media Freedom. In the midst of this legislative vacuum of the 1990s, media outlets including tabloid newspapers and politically affiliated television stations, burgeoned in Mongolia. Both the constitution and Law on Media Freedom were adopted in the zeitgeist of the 1990s, which overwhelmingly supported non-state media. By 2007, a UNESCO report counted up to 340 media outlets in the country (Nielsen et al. 2007). The Law on Media Freedom does not impose any societal and normative functions upon media, nor does it address how to transform the socialist state radio and television stations. At the same time, the state media still continued to play crucial roles because no law restrained the government from owning its own mass media. The development of a multifaceted media system can be seen in the increasing number of commercial television stations in Mongolia, as discussed below.

The Rise of Commercial Television

The first private television stations in Mongolia started in the "basement" of the national television station when professionals working there started to form independent studios and aired their programs over its network. The new Enterprise Law adopted in 1991 created a legal environment in which privately owned television stations like UBS, Channel 25, TV5, and TV9, along with foreign-owned, evangelical Eagle Broadcasting Corporation, were able to test and operate commercial television principles of garnering advertising money during their programs in the earlier years of commercial television between 1992 and 2005 (Unursaikhan 2019). Then, the mining boom in the country during 2008–12 and influx of foreign investment into the economy, which will be discussed in the next chapter, spilled over into the television business resulting in seven to twenty new television stations getting licensed each year. The number of commercial television stations grew in even greater amounts in the election years of 2008 and 2012, indicating growing partisanship and political influences. The number of television service licensees fluctuated: the CRC also revokes ten television licenses a year on average because of licensees' failure to fulfill the broadcast requirements, which, more often than not, is due to nonpayment of the small service fee of six hundred thousand tugriks (around 350 US dollars) and radio frequency fee of 150 thousand tugriks (seventy-five US dollars) (CRC 2013).

In the small media market of the three million people of Mongolia, around 135 television channels operate as of 2022 (PIM 2022). Ulaanbaatar, with its population of one million, leads the chart in media concentration with around fifty-five television channels. Even though this boom brought a growing number of local television stations such as *Lha, Eco,* and *Erdenet TV* to the countryside, it created an overly crowded and fragmented market for television businesses in the capital. The Mongolian media market has structural constraints typical to those in the small media states defined as media markets of between ten thousand and eighteen million inhabitants. These constraints are limited revenues in license fees, the shortage of advertising revenues, the scarcity of local quality content, and an international capital dependency, as media scholars explain (Puppis, 2009; Murphy, 2010). The scarcity of advertising dollars, financing resources, and talent push television businesses toward inexpensive and foreign programs and formats: daily news, talk shows, foreign syndicated shows and television series, sometimes violating international copyright law. In other words, the fragmentation in the television market in Mongolia scatters much-needed financing, talent, and other resources for producing quality programs in Mongolia, as well as for purchasing decent foreign programs and formats.

Along with these structural constraints, the financial dependency on the mining sector tax and the remnants of socialist institutional routines in media organizations also shape the television sector in Mongolia. Many of these television stations, excluding only a few television stations such as Mongol TV and the global syndicated network Bloomberg Mongolia, operate on shoestring budgets, and many of them are still mainly family-owned businesses. They do not have marketing or creative divisions, and, often, family owners do not understand the creative process involved in television businesses (interview with Unursaikhan, May 19, 2022). The Amendments to the Law on Culture of 2015 mandate that commercial broadcasters increase their Mongolian programs to 50 percent of their airtime (Amendments to the Law on Culture 2015). However, many small television stations cannot meet these requirements because they do not produce their own programs. Deficit financing necessary for television production, typical in the West, does not exist in the country, and there is no market for reruns of the syndicated programs in the Mongolian language.

The paradox of the increasing number of commercial television stations despite the small media market is explained by political affiliation and inexperienced business practices. There are many television stations, which only promote political candidates, especially during election times, and this situation erodes the principles of the television business. Khishigsuren, director of research at Maxima Consulting, explains the puzzle:

> There isn't a correlation between the number of television stations and the market size. We are the only organization that counts advertising dollars in the television business. It is around 30 million dollars a year.[3] There are too many television stations that operate on budgets of 500 thousand to one million dollars, which is nowhere close enough to produce any program. That is why television stations push translated content to audiences, their news programs are prepared only from the Government building, and many television stations broadcast stolen intellectual properties and air Korean dramas full of product placements. Around

3 Khishigsuren's estimates of the amount of advertising dollars correlate with the estimate by Friedrich Ebert Stiftung (2012), which was approximately twenty-million US dollars in 2012. If grey market transactions are added, which are usually 50 percent in the country, the amount becomes around thirty million (approximately sixty-billion tugrik).

> the time of the 2008 election, politicians thought they needed television channels to get elected to the Parliament. (interview with Khishigsuren, May 2016)

Even in 2022, many television stations remained politically dependent and financially inviable. Audience research, market analyses, and audiovisual policy are very important aspects of the television business, but both market analyses and audience research are limited in the country.

In 2019, the Mongolian Parliament adopted the long-awaited Law on Broadcasting, and the law is effective as of July 2020. The law was heavily lobbied by the strong political and commercial interests of television owners in that it created a mechanism for broadcast owners to financially benefit from the broadcast development fund in article 20. In the law, the state establishes and supports a broadcast development fund, which includes fees the multichannel operators would pay to broadcasters for carrying their programs, and this decision to distribute this fund is left to the newly established Mongolian Television Association, which conducts no audience or market research. The Press Institute of Mongolia (PIM) and Maxima Consulting are the only two groups conducting these types of research. Maxima Consulting has analyzed television ratings since 2007 based on data using people meter devices for one hundred families, and PIM monitors the public broadcaster's programs based on content analyses. Maxima Consulting's audience research was closed due to political and economic pressure. The law and how this law affects the market, and the public are discussed in more detail in chapter 4.

Transformation of State Television and Radio into Public Service Broadcasters and The Transition to Digital Television

In 2005, the government of Mongolia adopted the Law on Public Service Radio and Television that transformed the state-owned national radio and television station into a public service broadcaster. In Mongolia's postcommunist context, the term "the public interest" has not been clearly defined, and the media tend to amplify the voices of those in power and neglect the underserved, as I discuss below based on the cases of the transition of MNB to a public broadcaster and the transition of television stations to digital. The definition of public interest varies widely from country to country. The concept often involves the principles of programming diversity, a plurality of views, fostering locality, and serving the underserved (Napoli 2003). The transformation of state broadcasters to public broadcasters has been a long-term challenge because politicians do not relinquish their control and do not support MNB's independence.

During the seventy years of socialism, the interests of the public (*ард түмний эрх ашиг*) was the preamble of most laws proposed and approved by the communist party, which underplayed individual judgment, private thought, and private interests (*хувийн эрх сонирхол*). When the socialist era ended, the Mongolian Parliament shifted toward overwhelming support for commercial and liberal media, with little understanding of the media's social responsibility. Politicians conflated the interests of the ruling political factions with the public interest because MNB could advance political campaigns, and other politicians who owned television stations and commercial media themselves were reluctant to pass the Law on Public Service Radio and Television. Only under pressure from civil society organizations and international organizations did the Law on Public Service Radio and Television of 2005 get passed. This law has some forward-thinking provisions relating to the right to obtain information and the protection of sources by journalists.[4] However, the law did not guarantee MNB's political and economic independence from the government. The law limits MNB's advertisement and syndication and leaves the process of appointing the governing board and the executives in the hands of the government. The national council of MNB consists of fifteen members who are initially nominated by not-for-profit organizations. Then the president nominates four members, the parliament seven members, and the prime minister's cabinet four members. Because of Mongolia's political system, where the executive prime minister's cabinet is appointed by the winning parliamentary party, the ruling political party has a strong grip on MNB's oversight. Between 2021 and 2022, the MNB's national council's chair was changed twice, and the general director was changed three times. Furthermore, the law strictly limited MNB's advertising to 2 percent of airtime and left MNB dependent on government support. MNB has transformed into public service media but has many shortcomings according to a report edited by Lublinski et al. (2014), which evaluates the transitions of former state broadcasters to public service media in different countries. The lack of investigative reporting, low journalistic standards, a great amount of repetition of programs, and the dominance of government news sources are among the shortcomings

4 The statemen here is based on the interviews I conducted with several civil society experts in 2006. See Baasanjav 2008.

of MNB (Lublinski et al. 2014). Furthermore, MNB neither has a structure to carry out its public governance nor the mechanisms to respond to the public's complaints. These shortcomings became even clearer during the recent technological transformation of television from analog to digital.

When television systems were upgraded to digital transmission in Mongolia in 2016, the process was completed in a relatively short period compared to the US and European countries which went through the process earlier. Digital television brings better audio and video quality and uses radio frequencies more efficiently by compressing, meaning that six to eight channels can be transmitted over the radio frequency occupied by one channel in the analog system. The transition is complex technologically and socially because the rushed turnoff of analog television adversely affected disadvantaged groups who could not afford the technological upgrades. The countries that already transitioned to digital often compensated disadvantaged groups with state money or helped them to get set-top boxes. That is why in the United States, for example, the Telecommunications Act of 1996 mandated broadcasters to transition to digital television, and the process dragged on until 2009 (Taylor 2010). By 2016, the International Telecommunication Union (ITU) of the United Nations was setting a deadline for the remaining countries to switch over to digital (see ITU 2012). In an effort to meet the ITU deadline, the Mongolian agency that carried out the switchover, the Information Technology, Post and Telecommunications Authority (ITPTA), hurried it without clear policies concerning the social consequences. In 2015, one-third of Mongolians relied primarily on television for their news and information (PIM 2015), and the government ran out of the state monies planned for helping technologically and financially disadvantaged viewers. Approximately 120,000 households (14.5 percent of 823,000 households in Mongolia) could not afford set-top boxes or digital sets costing around thirty to forty US dollars. The public did not understand the transition to digital, and the grievances of those who lost their access to television were not heard. Their grievances were not heard by the relevant agencies, but only by the public broadcaster because the mandatory fees are collected from households (Baasanjav 2016). Little was stated in the Mongolian government program about improving program diversity, program quality, and advanced technological services for the public. The switchover also hurt small broadcasters operating in the countryside who did not have the means to purchase digital broadcast systems. The rushed switchover freed up valuable radio frequencies occupied by broadcasters, and then the government sold the freed digital dividends to mobile and next-generation technology companies.

Both transitions show the complexity of institutional changes that happen slowly and follow historical patterns. Mongolian institutions demonstrate the worst of both worlds—a continuity of socialist-era media control and an adaptation to neoliberalism. This situation also creates uncertainties about trust in the media.

Postcommunist Media Environment

The media market in Mongolia has not fully transitioned to an independent and healthy media market system in the last thirty years despite the dramatic increase in the proliferation of media outlets. The PIM (2022) reports the existence of around 486 media outlets: 64 newspapers, 46 magazines, 50 radio stations, 135 television stations, and 191 websites. When looking at the number of outlets and varieties, it appears that commercial media and media businesses have flourished. However, when looking into the economic principles of the commercial media and the normative media responsibilities media performs in Mongolian society, the media system still operates at the earlier stages of development. 73 percent of media outlets are privately owned, and 15 percent are owned by not-for-profit organizations, leaving 11 percent to state organization ownership and 1 percent to party ownership.

An increasing number of party-affiliated television stations, along with partisan journalism, show that the media's independence is still a challenge. Media businesses operate on the principle of balancing profit making with information services expected to benefit society. The electronic media model is widespread in a market economy and is often based on providing information/programs for audiences and, at the same time, packaging audiences for advertisers and other information providers. However, the Mongolian advertising market is not well established due to the small amount of market research in advertising and the small media market as I discussed above. Since 2005, Maxima Consulting has been the only organization that monitors advertising dollars in the media market. Despite the tripling of the economy due to the mining boom, the advertising market did not expand correspondingly but plateaued in 2012 at around thirty-million dollars a year (sixty billion tugriks).[5] When interviewed, Maxima Consulting executives elaborated:

5 Friedrich Ebert Stiftung (2012) estimated approximately twenty million in 2012.

> Advertising dollars on the market have not increased since 2007 and remained at around 49 million dollars a year despite the fact that many foreign companies were interested in Mongolia's mining boom. We count advertisers' spendings, which include all media from newspapers to television to social media. There was another foreign study in 2012, which estimated an even lower amount, around 20 million dollars. But our counting includes barter trading. It is a paradox that the number of television stations and airtime has increased while advertising dollars remained the same over the recent years. You get puzzled about how they get funded. The reasons for stagnant advertising dollars are a small and unestablished market and political and government interference into the market. Since 2017, big foreign advertisers left, and nowadays, a list of top advertisers is led by the Police Department and the Health Department, not Proctor & Gamble and Coca-Cola. Besides, since 2017, advertising dollars predominantly go to social media, mostly to Facebook and Google ... Media owners don't even understand how and what they lost. They are just happy to get money from the government mostly. (interview with Khishigsuren and Enkhjargal, May 10, 2022)

Khishigsuren and Enkhjargal of Maxima Consulting compare the Mongolian market to that of Kazakhstan and Uzbekistan, the former socialist countries where international ad agencies and sales houses have their branches. With only 3.3 million people, the Mongolian media market has structural constraints typical to those in the small media states (defined as media markets of between ten thousand to eighteen million inhabitants), such as limited revenues in license fees, a shortage of advertising revenues, a scarcity of local quality content, and an international capital dependency as discussed in Puppis (2009) and Murphy (2010). Since the fall of the socialist state, the Mongolian media market has taken in less money from international advertisers compared to other Asian postcommunist states. International advertisers and sales houses have their Moscow and Kazakhstan branches to cover Mongolia due to the cultural similarities of using the Cyrillic alphabet and the communistic past. International ad agencies like WPP and Omnicom do not operate in Mongolia because, like the television market, the ads market is constrained by the small market and high operational costs. Besides, audience and marketing research, which counts eyeballs, competition for programs, and content distribution, is scarce in Mongolia (Baasanjav 2016). The decreased revenue from international and domestic ads led to a situation where Mongolian government organizations became the biggest funder of the media. Excessive government funding into the media market erodes the advertising and television markets simultaneously.

Media professor Unursaikhan, who wrote a book on commercial television and worked in one of the television stations, explains how television outlets in Mongolia made most of their money during the Mongolian election years while operating on barely sustaining budgets during nonelection years. Because politicians understand the power of television, half of parliamentarians own television stations with their families or cronies. But they understand little about the business of television. Unursaikhan goes on to say:

> Most television stations have only news and program divisions and do not have marketing teams or producers. If you want to create a program, the owners say, "find your own sponsor." One person cannot produce news, create programs, and find talent and financers. Owners pay little to professionals and journalists and do not incentivize creativity or teamwork. They default on their employees' health insurance or social security payments. They barely fill out airtime with news and talk shows. There is a saying that if you don't have economic freedom, you don't have freedom (interview with Unursaikhan, May 18, 2022).

Even though the proliferation of television stations has occurred, they are neither economically nor editorially independent from the entrenched power of politician owners. Unursaikhan brings up the financial dependency of television stations on windfall profits of elections and their dependency on financiers to create television programs. Because of these tangled political and economic dependencies, commercial television stations are filled with sponsored programs, financial muddling, and political dependency. People who sponsor programs silence critical news involving sponsors' businesses. Television also creates very powerful lobby groups that twist policies in their interests. Examples of powerful lobbies include the selection of national broadcasters that are supposed to be competitively selected and the mapping of broadcast zones that are supposed to be open and public. I will discuss how these lobby groups influenced the Law on Broadcasting of 2019 later in chapter 4. Below, I discuss how new digital media are changing the television market players and businesses. Maxima Consulting interviewees acknowledge that by 2016 in Mongolia the more significant portion of advertising dollars already go to digital and social media rather than legacy media.

Media Convergence and Proliferation of Digital Platforms

Digital convergence in Mongolia has accelerated in recent years. PIM (2022) lists twenty-two online television sites, including mnb.mn, bloombergtv.mn, mongoltv.mn, eagle.mn, tv5.mn, tv9.mn, and television subscription sites such as looktv.mn, and motv.mn live cast forty or more television stations with program guides. The number of online news and entertainment sites has grown to 191, including mglradio.com and gogo.mn that webcast digitalized content over the internet and mobile platforms (PIM 2022).

Media convergence refers not only to technological changes but also spills out to business practices of communication networks and their regulations by the government. In many countries, the consequences of media convergence led to a frenzy of consolidation among media outlets (McChesney 1999; Mueller 1999). The transition to digital television in 2016 in Mongolia, for example, was primed by media convergence internationally. One of the explanations the Mongolian government gave when it cut out the money dedicated to helping poorer groups purchase digital set-top boxes and digital television sets was that consumers have different technological platforms and sets to choose from, and the government did not want to interfere with the choices. Many households (around 30–40 percent of the households) at the time of the initiation of the digital transition were already viewing television over cable, satellite, wireless cable, and the internet (also called Internet Protocol television or IPTV). An increasing number of available digital platforms reduced the number of people who fully rely on over-the-air television. The number of viewers receiving television over alternative platforms reached 669,881 in 2014, of which 15 percent use cable, 48 percent satellite, 18 percent wireless cable, and 19 percent use IPTV (CRC 2014). By the time of the analog switch off or digital transition, the number of television channels was around 140, of which sixteen were broadcast nationwide, sixty-one operated in Ulaanbaatar, and the rest operated in the countryside locally (Baasanjav 2016).

The convergence among different platforms like IPTV, cable, and satellite creates new possibilities for public interest services. This convergence brought benefits but should be assessed holistically in media laws and policy. I will discuss in a later chapters how, unlike European and other countries that implemented diligent policies for ensuring equality among different platforms in the converged media space (Murphy 2010; Wheeler 2012), the Mongolian program lacks such a policy. Clear examples of the undesirable outcomes of the lack of understanding of the relationship between broadcast, cable, and IPTV can be seen in the implementation of the recently adopted

Law on Broadcasting of 2019. When the Law on Broadcasting required cable companies to pay small fees to contribute to the national programming fund for carrying television programs, as I will discuss in detail in chapter 4, cable companies increased their subscription fees. This way IPTV and cable operators passed the burden onto their unsuspecting subscribers. It is also possible that lower quality and cheaply produced programs are kept for digital terrestrial television networks, especially in the countryside, creating content duality. Platform inequality between terrestrial television and cable companies exists and, without proper regulations, this situation hurts the unsuspecting public.

New on-demand and time-shifted platforms like IPTV can increase opportunities for educational services. One example is the Open Network for Education initiative (one.mn),[6] which offers access to an online collection of more than two-thousand micro lectures in Mongolian on subjects including mathematics, history, English, and traditional Mongolian script. This initiative partners with the US Khan Academy (www.khanacademy.org) and the Ministry of Education, Culture and Science (MECS) of Mongolia, and provides translation of instructional resources developed by the Khan Academy and instructional videos independently developed by local teachers via YouTube. The national policy for online education on social media platforms like YouTube and Facebook in the local language can make these services distinct from millions of other online programs and YouTube videos. These videos are concomitantly available over Univision, an IPTV on-demand service in Ulaanbaatar.

Social Media

Young people, journalists, and civil society activists in Mongolia utilize Facebook Messenger and Facebook pages mainly because "the whole of Mongolia is on Facebook," as one of the journalists who participated in the focus group interviews in 2019 summarized. The Facebook Basic project has replaced basic telecommunications services in the countryside and cities so that "when you message someone on Facebook, the person always gets back to you one way or another," according to the journalist. In the last couple of years, Facebook Messenger has diffused into Mongolian society, even in the countryside, where traditional media and telecommunications services were scarce.

6 The website one.mn reroutes now to https://mn.khanacademy.org/.

Mongolians revere YouTube's free tutorials for educational purposes, Facebook Messenger's communicative features, and Twitter's (now X's) virality for information dissemination, and those are the platforms they most frequently use. Social media platforms like Facebook enable viral informational sharing, reaching out to many people and mobilizing them effectively on various issues, from gender equality to corruption.

Social media campaigns for rock bands, gender causes, investigative reports, or other social "swarming" are relatively new to Mongolia, but there have been apparent developments in this area. Mongolians felt a sense of being involved in global affairs when they stopped the abduction of Turkish school educator Veysel Akçay, whom Turkish President Erdoğan ordered to be abducted for an alleged connection to the Gülen movement, which was linked to the coup plot to overthrow the Turkish government in 2018. The educator lived in Ulaanbaatar for a long time and was loved by students and teachers at the school. They "swarmed" the airport and demanded that the Mongolian authorities stop the abduction jet after the news about his abduction was swiftly shared on Facebook and Twitter.

Social media's ease of use and affordability enable young people to create Facebook groups like Women for Change and drive changes on social issues. Women for Change is a not-for-profit organization that started in 2010 as a Facebook group of sixteen women discussing gender inequality in the country. A year later, the group became a not-for-profit organization that promotes gender equality and fights against sexual assault, harassment, and domestic violence. The group page has sixty-six thousand members comprised mostly of students (Baasanjav 2020), and the popularity of the group on social media even compelled the minister of education to sit down with them on sexual harassment issues amidst the minister's denial of sexual harassment in universities.

In 2022, investigative journalist Budragchaa broke a story of the corruption and public fund abuse case by the principal of a reputable joint Mongolian-Russian School in Ulaanbaatar. The journalist employed a crowdfunding mechanism to support his investigative reports when he went live on Facebook to report on the case. He raised 8.1 million tugriks from the public, many of whom knew him from the previous investigative reports with live.tv and contributed three, seven, or thirty US dollars. His previous investigative story on the sexual harassment and physical abuse case surrounding the soccer coach of Mongolia's under-15 girls' team broke on YouTube in 2019 and the story was picked up by the *Guardian* when he was working for live.tv (Aarons and Molina 2021). In the latest story, he documented how school principal Soronzon benefitted by giving the school's soccer field to a construction company and, in return, received an apartment. She also paid the company 340,000 US dollars a year from the school budget. Over her thirty-year career, Soronzon established an influential network of board members, alumni, and parents, including the deputy minister, the deputy police chief, influential judges, and police officers. These powerful people fended off her criminal case by dismissing it, while the principal threatened and even tried to bribe the journalist. Not only was she not charged, she instead filed five libel and defamation cases against Budragchaa. All defamation cases against him were dropped because his report was sufficiently backed by facts and evidence (Baasanjav et al. 2024).

The above examples show the viral, hyperlinked, and interactive affordances of social media that help organizations and individuals act immediately and connectedly. People, in general, have a favorable perception of social media when I discuss possible pitfalls of social media with interviewees in Mongolia. One of the leaders of Women for Change said in 2019 that Facebook allows them tactical swarming possibilities when organizing an event, and they were able to respond quickly to unseen circumstances during a protest. She also added that Facebook is not always the best place for explaining complex human rights issues at length.

The embedded logic of social media promoting virality and publicity compels a group to create somewhat quickly "consumable" content for an audience, which might cater toward the "trivialization" of complex human rights issues. Social media scholars argue that people increasingly post safe political content to not be attacked or called out. Furthermore, when a person's active audience differs from the "imagined audience" on social media, a "context collapse" occurs (boyd 2010). Posts for close friends might be seen by parents or authorities, and insider's conversations could be read by an unexpected audience. Context collapse contributes to the reasons why people do not engage deeply on Facebook (Galis and Neumayer 2016; Richez et al. 2020).

As social media deeply permeate all spheres of Mongolian society, the differences in the levels and depth of use are widening due to the differences in socioeconomic status, education, cultural background, and media literacy in ways similar to the US and other countries. These differences in use and socioeconomic status of social media users also bring forth the importance of focusing on "platform-specific affordances" (Bucher and Helmond 2017; Poell and Van Dijk 2015). Scholars of technology and design studies adopted the term "affordances" to the study of social media and elaborated upon the concept to refer to a range of possible actions linked to features of a specific social media platform. The term initially comes from the field of ecological psychology and refers to a perceived range of possible actions to an animal in a certain environmental terrain (Bucher and Helmond 2017).

There is a perceived hierarchy in terms of platforms among Mongolians, in which Facebook is seen as more engaging than Twitter (X), but has a less-valued "mass" base, whereas Twitter is seen as having a more professional or selective base. On Mongolian Twitter, a small number of active users post similar to the findings in other countries (Arceneaux and Dinu 2018; Matuszewski and Szabó 2019). A leader of a women's not-for-profit organization mentioned that in 2019, her organization "might appear not very professional" because "people ask why we do not have a website after 10 years of existence; but exist only on Facebook" (interview with Anu, 2019). Social media further exacerbate social divides by deepening the knowledge gap and increasing the epistemological asymmetry, as Reviglio and Agosti (2020) and Zuboff (2019) discuss. The lesser the education level, the greater the limitations upon the person's social networks because people tend to attract mostly similar-minded people in their media circles. With more people having a social media presence, an asymmetry in the quality of information people read rather than access deepens social stratification. Furthermore, the traditional digital divides between the city and the countryside, as well as between the better-off and the resource-poor institutions, are increasing. Libraries and cultural organizations in the countryside and the outskirts of cities do not enjoy the same access and inclusive possibilities because internet access in the countryside and outskirts of Ulaanbaatar is very limited.

Many people believe in the inevitable benefits of social media, as Zuboff (2019) observed in the United States, and only a few Mongolians are cognizant of the information collection and other surveillance on social media platforms. Many who are aware think that content and interactions that occur in the Mongolian language are of no use to Facebook. While laws do not delineate who has the right to collect, aggregate and disseminate personal data, companies and public organizations have increasingly started to use surveillance technologies such as video cameras and fingerprint readers. Schools and daycare centers first started setting up cameras at the request of parents who were concerned about the corporal punishment of young kids by daycare workers and schoolteachers. New criminal laws now admit video recordings as evidence. In the summer of 2019, 1,200 public buses in Ulaanbaatar were equipped with video cameras. Banks and mobile phone operators issue loans and open accounts without much paperwork using fingerprint authentication.

While banks and mobile operators use these biometric technologies and data, the police do not have criminal databases, nor do they utilize these technologies in crime scenes. My interviewees pointed out that the discriminatory use of surveillance technologies mostly benefits bigger businesses that have resources to utilize surveillance and behavioral datafication as Zuboff (2019) warned. Meanwhile, education and not-for profit organizations lack resources and expertise to utilize information databases and to defend themselves against cyberattacks and hacks. The University of the Humanities in Ulaanbaatar lost educational sources and training materials to a cyberattack when the school transferred its servers to the servers of Univision, one of the major cable and internet providers in the capital. The university lost much of its educational content, and the legal case they filed against Univision lasted for years. Cyber attackers are increasingly exploiting the internet's security vulnerabilities in the digital eras, while laws and protection mechanisms prohibiting these kinds of exploitations are rudimentary in Mongolia.

Conclusion

This chapter historicizes the media development in Mongolia and contextualizes changing informational spheres within the country's dramatic political and social changes. When politicians and the public, many of whom grew up with the monolithic propagandistic media, transitioned to a chaotic, liberal, and profit-oriented media landscape, they were dismayed by the multiplicity of the forms and motives of commercial media. The ideological vacuum and economic hardships following the Soviet collapse left the country without legal and regulatory frameworks to protect the rights of its citizens and the press. Political and economic changes created a context for many Mongolians that made it hard to make sense of information coming from multiple outlets, including social media. I showed how the notion of the public interest was almost misinterpreted in a way that benefitted the ruling elites when the Law on Media Freedom was adopted. The examples of the digital transition of television and the transformation of national television to a public service broadcaster also show that, while the government declared success, some disadvantaged groups were left unaccounted for in the state policies and their implementations. It appears that there was no grievance vehicle for those left behind. The principles of inclusivity and diversity of audience in the programs and the workforce were not stated in media laws and policies, and this situation already hurt the most vulnerable people.

Digital convergence and technological advances worldwide are also catching up with Mongolia amidst its changes to democracy and a market economy. Relatively new legal and state institutions emulate international laws and policies in adopting technological advances and social media; however, the particulars of Mongolia's context are not reflected in the state's policies, laws, and business practices. International policy and regulations coordinate and cover technological aspects while leaving social and cultural implications to the local authorities. A piecemeal approach to regulations of a variety of converging technologies, including cable television and satellite and mobile phones, treats platforms differently, and this situation leaves a loophole in technological laws and regulations. Politicians' understanding of the role of media and their expectations molded during the socialist era remain and continue to affect emergent media and social media. On the other hand, the public during the socialist surveillance time did not engage critically with the media and did not expect social responsibilities from the media. This uncritical acceptance of monolithic socialist media to some extent, dovetails with the people's uncritical expectations of social media platforms, as though socialist propaganda was replaced by benevolent social media platforms. Because local authorities do so little to make media policies and regulations, this vacuum should probably be filled by international policies and laws.

Work Cited

Aarons, Ed and Romain Molina. 2021. "Fifa Criticised Over Handling of Sexual Harassment Case in Mongolia." *The Guardian*, Oct. 21. https://www.theguardian.com/football/2021/oct/21/fifa-criticised-over-handling-of-sexual-harassment-case-in-mongolia.

Amendments to the Law on Culture [Соёлын Тухай Хуульд Нэмэлт Оруулах Тухай]. 2015.

Arceneaux, Phillip C. and Lucian F. Dinu. 2018. "The Social Mediated Age of Information: Twitter and Instagram as Tools for Information Dissemination in Higher Education." *New Media & Society* 20 (11): 4155–76.

Batbayar, Bat-Erdene (Baabar). 1999. *Twentieth Century Mongolia.* Translated by D. Sühjargalmaa, S. Burenbayar, H. Hulan, and N. Tuya. Edited by C. Kaplonski. White Horse Press.

Baasanjav, Undrah B. 2016. "The Public Interest and Transition to Digital Television in Mongolia." *International Journal of Digital Television* 7 (1): 7–22.

———. 2020. "Social Media and Credibility: Civil Society Organizations in Mongolia." In *SMSociety'20: International Conference on Social Media and Society,* edited by Anatoliy Gruzd, Philip Mai, Raquel Recuero, Ángel Hernández-García, Chei Sian Lee, James Cook et al., 230–7. Association for Computing Machinery. https://doi.org/10.1145/3400806.3400833.

Baasanjav, Undrah B., Poul E. Nielsen, and Munkhmandakh Myagmar. 2024. "Patronage Media in Post-Communist Mongolia." *Central European Journal of Communication* 17 (2(36)): 247–67. https://doi.org/10.51480/1899-5101.17.2(36).573.

boyd, Danah. 2010. "Social Network Sites as Networked Publics: Affordances, Dynamics, and Implications." In *Networked Self: Identity, Community, and Culture on Social Network Sites*, edited by Zizi Papacharissi. 39–58. London, UK: Routledge.

Bucher, Taina and Anne Helmond. 2017. "The Affordances of Social Media Platforms." In *The SAGE Handbook of Social Media*, edited by Jean Burgess, Alice Marwick, and Thomas Poell, 233–53. SAGE.

Buyandelger, Manduhai. 2022. *A Thousand Steps to Parliament: Constructing Electable Women in Mongolia.* The University of Chicago Press.

Coast, David and Jo Fox. 2015. "Rumour and Politics." *History Compass* 13 (5): 222–34.

Coleman, Stephen and Ildiko Kaposi. 2006. "New Democracies, New Media: What's New? A Study of E-Participation Projects in Third-Wave Democracies." *E-Governance Academy.* https://ega.ee/wp-content/uploads/2015/03/Coleman_handbook.pdf.

CRC. 2013. "Радио Давтамжийн Ашиглалт, Үйлчилгээний Төлбөрийн Хэмжээ" [Radio Frequency Usage and Service Fees].

CRC. 2014. "2014 Year-End Key Indicators for the Sector." [Харилцаа холбооны салбарын 2014 оны жилийн эцсийн үндсэн үзүүлэлтүүд]. https://manage.crc.gov.mn/articles/slug10039/en.

Empson, Rebecca M. 2020. *Subjective Lives and Economic Transformations in Mongolia: Life in the Gap.* UCL Press. https://doi.org/10.14324/111.9781787351462.

Friedrich Ebert Stiftung. 2012. *Asian Media Barometer: Mongolia 2012.* https://library.fes.de/pdf-files/bueros/asia-media/10293.pdf.

Galis, Vasilis and Christina Neumayer. 2016. "Laying Claim to Social Media by Activists: A Cyber-Material *Détournement*." *Social Media + Society* 2 (3). https://doi.org/10.1177/2056305116664360.

Holmes, Leslie. 1997. *Post-Communism: An Introduction.* Duke University Press.

ITU. 2012. *Guidelines for the Transition from Analog to Digital Broadcasting.* https://www.itu.int/ITU-D/tech/digital_broadcasting/project-dbasiapacific/Digital-Migration-Guidelines_EV7.pdf.

Jakubowicz, Karol. 2011. "Public Service Broadcasting: Product (and Victim?) of Public Policy." In *The Handbook of Global Media and Communication*, edited by Robin Mansell and Mark Raboy, 210–29. Blackwell.

Kaplonski, Chistopher. 2004. *Truth, History and Politics in Mongolia: Memory of Heroes*. Routledge.

Lublinski, Jan, Merjam Wakili, and Petra Berner, eds. 2014. *In the Service of the Public: Functions and Transformations of Media in Developing Countries*. Deutsche Welle. http://www.internews.org/sites/default/files/resources/DW-akademie-2015-01_In_the_service_of_the_public.pdf.

Matuszewski, Paweł and Gabriella Szabó. 2019. "Are Echo Chambers Based on Partisanship? Twitter and Political Polarity in Poland and Hungary." *Social Media + Society* 5 (2). https://doi.org/10.1177/2056305119837671.

Maxima Consulting. 2014. "2014 Оны Телевиз Үзэлтийн Судалгааны Тайлан" [2014 Television Audience Survey Report]. Unpublished Report. https://maxima.mn/2014-tam-tailan.

McChesney, Robert. 1999. *Rich Media, Poor Democracy: Communication Politics in Dubious Times*. University of Illinois Press.

Mueller, Milton. 1999. "Digital Convergence and Its Consequences." *Javnost—The Public* 6 (3): 11–27.

Murphy, Kenneth. 2010. "Digital Television Policy and Regulatory Neutrality in Small Western States: Ireland, Greece, Finland, Austria and New Zealand. *International Journal of Digital Television* 1 (2): 155–71.

Napoli, Philip. 2003. "The Public Interest Obligations Initiative: Lost in the Digital Television Shuffle." *Journal of Broadcasting and Electronic Media* 47 (1): 153–6.

Nielsen, P. E., Redl, A., & Ziyasheva, D. (2007). *The Mongolian Media Landscape: Sector Analysis.* Unesco. https://pure.au.dk/portal/en/publications/the-mongolian-media-landscape-sector-analysis

Press Institute of Mongolia. 2015. *Mongolian Media Today.* Ulaanbaatar: The Press Institute.

Press Institute of Mongolia. 2022. *Mongolian Media Today.* Ulaanbaatar: The Press Institute.

Poell, Thomas and José van Dijck. 2015. "Social Media and Activist Communication." In *The Routledge Companion to Alternative and Community Media*, edited by Chris Atton, 527–37. Routledge.

Puppis, Manuel. 2009. "Media Regulation in Small States." *The International Communications Gazette* 71 (1–2): 7–17.

Reviglio, Urbano and Claudio Agosti. 2020. "Thinking Outside the Black-Box: The Case For 'Algorithmic Sovereignty' in Social Media." *Social Media + Society* 6 (2). https://doi.org/10.1177/2056305120915613.

Richez, Emmanuelle, Vincent Raynauld, Abunya Agi, and Arief B. Kartolo. 2020. "Unpacking the Political Effects of Social Movements with a Strong Digital Component: The case of #IdleNoMore in Canada." *Social Media + Society* 6 (2). https://doi.org/10.1177/2056305120915588.

Sanders, Alan J. K. 1987. *Mongolia: Politics, Economics and Society*. Frances Pinter.

Sneath, David. 2010. "Political Mobilization and the Construction of Collective Identity in Mongolia." *Central Asian Survey* 29 (3): 251–67.

Sparks, Colin and Anna Reading. 1998. *Communism, Capitalism and the Mass Media*. SAGE.

Taylor, Gregory. 2010. "Shut-off: The Digital Television Transition in the United States and Canada." *Canadian Journal of Communication* 35 (1): 7–26.

Unursaikhan, Tugj. 2019. *Mongolian Commercial Television: History, Theory and Practice* [Монголын арилжааны телевизүүд: түүх, онол, арга зүй]. Ulaanbaatar: UdamSoyol.

Voltmer, Katrin. 2013. *The Media in Transitional Democracies*. Polity.

Wheeler, Mark. 2012. "European Union State Aid, Public Subsidies and Analogue Switch-Off/Digital Switchover." *International Journal of Digital Television* 3 (1): 7–12.

Zuboff, Shoshana. 2019. *The Age of Surveillance Capitalism: The Fight for a Human Future at the New Frontier of Power*. Public Affairs.

3. Economic Reality: Mining, Debt, Media, and Information Markets

Abstract: This chapter explores the confluence of the informational economy and extractive capitalism in Mongolia over the twenty-first century. Media outlets have proliferated, partly thanks to the growth of foreign investment in the mining sector. I discuss how mining contributes to the country's debt accumulation and environmental degradation in comparison to the ICT sector, utilizing the ratios between the direct investment and the contributions to the country's GDP following Thomas Piketty's (2014) political economy analysis. The money from mining feeds back into media institutions that cover the industries. I argue that the formation of a national epistemic community in the ICT sector in the late 1990s and the lack of such a community in the mining sector made differences in how the two sectors contributed to Mongolian society.

Keywords: extractive mining, national dept, mining discourse, ICT sector, direct investment, Thomas Piketty, and epistemic community

Media development and the information sector have rapidly accelerated in Mongolia in the last twenty years, partly thanks to the growth of foreign investment in the mining sector and the export of minerals. The mining boom in the country during 2008–13 tripled the economy, lured in big multinational companies like Rio Tinto and Ivanhoe Mines, and increased the public's use of communication technology, as discussed in chapter 1. In recent years, the dominant economic extractive sector has started to define the economic outlook of Mongolia directly and influence its political and cultural life indirectly. Mongolians, along with international mining corporations, explored and exploited the mineral resources of copper, gold, coal, oil, and uranium extensively, increasing the country's GDP to 13.85-billion American dollars in 2020 from 1.35 billion in 2000 (World Bank 2020). The

Undrah Baasanjav, *Information Society and Media Development in Modern Mongolia*.
Taylor & Francis Group, 2025
DOI: 10.5117/9789463729888_CH03

World Bank (2021) estimates that mining accounts for more than 80 percent of Mongolia's exports and 25 percent of its GDP (World Bank 2021).

As the defining economic sector, mining dominates public discourse, while the money from the sector spills into the media market and organizations via legitimate and illegitimate means. Will the income brought by mining help the country overcome the resource dependency, environmental degradation, and foreign debt accumulated over the years? This chapter explores the economic dependency on mining in relation to the government's aspirational rhetoric of transitioning to an information society. This chapter provides an analysis of how the confluences of the informational economy and extractive capitalism occurred in Mongolia over the twenty-first century. At the same time, the relationship between the government and foreign companies has become a source of tension and, to some extent, contributes to corruption and nationalistic sentiment.

Political and Economic Discourse on Mining and the Mineral State

The 2020 report of the International Council on Mining and Metals (ICMM 2020) ranks Mongolia third in its Mining Contribution Index (MCI) based on the weight the mining industry plays in the national economy. According to the report, metallic mineral and coal production accounted for 37.6 percent of the country's GPD in 2018, and mineral rent constituted 28.9 percent of the GDP. Around four hundred large mining companies led by the Oyu Tolgoi copper and gold mine, Erdenet copper and molybdenum mine, and the coal mine in Tavan Tolgoi, as well as artisanal and small-scale mining (ASM), produce 85.6 percent of the total exports, marking Mongolia as a resource-dependent country. The geographical proximity of Mongolian mines to the fast-growing markets in China and Russia also appeals to big mining corporations. Over the last fifteen years, major mining companies such as British-Australian Rio Tinto and Canadian-based Ivanhoe Mines dramatically increased their investments.

Immediately after the collapse of the Soviet system in the 1990s, Mongolian politicians started to dream of becoming a "mineral state," mainly due to the dire economic situation. Mining exploration and the exploitation of iron, fluorite, uranium, and coal started in Mongolia with Soviet investment during World War II and the following years, when metal and iron were in great demand for military purposes. In 1949, a joint Soviet-Mongolian Metal Group was established, and since then it conducted mineral expeditions and land cadastral mapping. Mardai's uranium ore, Nalaikh's coal, Modot's tin, Berkh's fluorite, and Erdenet's copper and molybdenum mines were discovered, built or rebuilt with Soviet investments. During the socialist era, geological surveys, also known as cadastral information, revealing land wealth and resources, were not disclosed to the public (MRPAM, n.d.). Mardai's uranium ore was classified as a secret site until the Soviets left in the 1990s, leaving the town empty, while Erdenet's copper and molybdenum mines became one of the biggest copper mines in Central Asia.

The first elected president of Mongolia, Punsalmaa Ochirbat, was a geologist himself, and he initiated the Gold and Petroleum Program to overcome the economic collapse of the Soviet bloc. Political leaders, including Ochirbat and the first prime minister after the collapse of the communist party Dashiin Byambasüren made the argument that mining projects were necessary to lure "third neighbor" companies from Canada, Australia, and America to invest in Mongolia, thus diminishing the overpowering influences of China and Russia and preserving political independence (Bumochir 2018). The first mining companies coming to the country, such as Boroo Gold of Australia, were enticed with extremely favorable terms, including full tax exemption for the first three years and a 50 percent tax reduction over the next three years. Around that time, geological surveys and information on minerals documented by the Soviet-led GeoFund became available to the public. Ironically, the first mining companies started their geological explorations with already existing Soviet-championed studies that were kept hidden from the public. Mines usually undergo several phases of exploration, feasibility and planning, construction, operation, closure, and post-closure (Cane et al. 2015). How much explorative investment was spent by these companies is not known at all. After the Soviets left, the documentation of mineral resources became available, including information on easily washable gold dusts and particles in river basins, also known as placer gold. This started Mongolia's gold rush and widespread "ninja" or artisanal mining.[1] This situation of secretly kept geological surveys, tax exemptions for foreign mines, and the emergence of artisanal miners invoked the distributional justice discussions in the media for a long period.

The discourse of mining dominates the media during Mongolian elections. During the recent 2021 presidential election, the president-elect Ukhnaagiin Khürelsükh of the ruling Mongolian People's Party (MPP) ran on the slogan "Mongolia Owns Its Wealth" (*Баялагтаа эзэн Монгол*) and received

1 High, 2017; also watch webcast "Mining in Mongolia 'Doesn't Come Without Environmental or Social Risks,'" accessed August 29, 2022 at https://asiasociety.org/switzerland/webcast-mining-mongolia-doesnt-come-without-environmental-or-social-risks.

67.8 percent of the total vote, while the second-closest presidential candidate, Dangaasürengiin Enkhbat of The Right Person Electorate Coalition, ran on the slogan "Mongolia Can" (*Монгол Чадна*) and received 20.3 percent of the total vote. The Democratic Party's candidate Sodnomzunduin Erdene, whose slogan "Mongolia without Dictatorship" (*Дарангуйлалгүй Монгол*) did not reverberate with the voters, came in third, receiving 6 percent of the total vote, close to the percentage of votes cast blank. The president-elect's political rhetoric of prioritizing the management of the mines received more popular support compared to Enkhbat's campaign slogan prioritizing human capital in the country. The new president and former prime minister Khürelsükh, in his campaign "The Agreement for Justice and Development," put forward a number of oil production and natural gas pipeline projects, as well as the improvement of previous contracts with big mines like Oyu Tolgoi (OT) and Tavan Tolgoi (TT). The 2021 presidential election campaign slogans got traction in the media by discussing the relationship between global capital and the human capability for development. In chapter 1, I discussed how Dangaasürengiin Enkhbat started internet services in the country. His supporters, mostly in Ulaanbaatar and the urban areas, rallied behind his more human-focused campaign and his technology expertise partly because his platform messages alluded to the diversification of the economy beyond extractive mines.

Since the mining boom, politicians have used mining contracts with foreign companies to evoke nationalistic sentiments during the elections. The MPP—the current majority in the parliament—and newly elected president Ukhnaagiin Khürelsükh campaigned on the renegotiation of the underground expansion contracts for OT to improve the condition for Mongolia. OT is one of the world's largest copper-gold deposits, located eighty kilometers from the Chinese north border, and is estimated to hold over 8.8 million tons of copper and 262 tons of gold (World Bank 2021). The controversies surrounding OT's exploitation contract has caused friction between Rio Tinto and the Mongolian government in recent years.

The original contract for OT—also infamously known as the Dubai contract—signed in 2009 by the Mongolian Government then ruled by the Democratic Party and Rio Tinto, one of the world's biggest multinationals in mining, has been contested in several international courts of arbitration as well as in Mongolian courts. The Mongolian side contests that the original contract gave too many advantages to Ivanhoe mines, then the owner of OT now owned by Rio Tinto, over the country's interests (Munkhchimeg and Lewis 2019). Mongolia's Independent Authority Against Corruption (IAAC) arrested a couple of former prime ministers and several cabinet members on charges of abuse of power in relation to mineral resource contracts in 2018–9. One of the officials is the former finance minister Sangajav Bayartsogt, who was one of the signatories of the 2009 contract. Investigative journalist Lkhagva Erdene of Mongol TV, who worked on the Offshore Leaks Database in the famous Panama Papers, along with the International Consortium of Investigative Journalists (ICIJ), revealed Bayartsogt's offshore accounts, and he was charged with corruption and was convicted. Under these circumstances, the Mongolian Tax Authority (MTA) issued tax dispute statements in international arbitration on the tax amount received from OT for the years 2013–5 and 2016–8 for the amount of 155 million and 228 million dollars, respectively (Turquoise Hill Resources 2021). MTA claims that the initial contracts and the underground development financing plan do not benefit Mongolia and also referred to improper payments to government officials in 2009 that granted Rio Tinto advantageous terms. Turquoise Hill, in return, claimed that they fully paid taxes according to the contracts signed previously with the Mongolian government. In 2019, the parliament of Mongolia issued resolution 92 to improve the implementation of the initial contract, the investment agreement, and the Underground Mine Development and Financing Plan of 2015. The underground mining started in 2022 after some agreements were achieved between the two parties.

Another mining contract, which was at the center of the parliamentary election of 2016, concerns the copper-molybdenum mine Erdenet, which used to be a joint mine with Russia since 1978. Then Prime Minister Chimediin Saikhanbileg announced to journalists on the pre-election night of June 28, 2016, that Mongolia bought Russia's 49 percent shares in the mine and that Mongolia would be the sole owner of the biggest copper mine in Mongolia (Lkhagva and Radchenko 2016). The Erdenet mine was first explored by a Mongol-Czech geological expedition in 1963 and by Soviet geologists in 1964–8. In 1973, the Mongolian People's Republic and the Soviet Union signed a joint 50/50 partnership agreement, and the mine started operating in 1978. The mine produces around 530,000 tons of copper and five-thousand tons of molybdenum concentrates used for steel alloys on average each year (MCC, n.d.). Depending on the international market price of copper, the company sales make up to 12 percent of the GDP, and in 2019 it accounted for 8 percent of government tax revenues for the country (Erdenejargal 2020). The mining development also led to the creation of Erdenet town (Erdenet in Mongolian means "treasure") and a railway connecting the town to the Trans-Siberian Railway between China and Russia. When the Soviet Union ended, the Mongolian side increased its share to 51 percent, leaving 49 percent to the Russian state-owned company Rostec. The socialist-era trade terms of copper with Russia were not beneficial for the company, but the post-Soviet-era sales revenues for Erdenet have greatly improved.

In 2016, almost unknown to the public, the new Mongolian Copper Corporation (MCC) raised the funds and bought Russia's shares worth four-hundred-million dollars—a much higher price than the actual assets of the company—to entice the Russian side to cash in its shares, and the deal was announced the night before the election (Lkhagva and Radchenko 2016). MCC borrowed two-hundred-million dollars from the Trade and Development Bank of Mongolia and raised another two hundred million on its own. Who the buyer was and why Vladimir Putin agreed to the deal that sold one of the major Russian strategic assets in Mongolia were among many unanswered questions surrounding this secret deal. According to the investigative expose by Lkhagva and Radchenko (2016), this stunt of the prime minister's backfired for the ruling Democratic Party (DP) and the party sweepingly lost in 2016. Saikhanbileg himself lost his seat in the parliament and the prime minister's office. The deal went through a lengthy legal battle involving the Supreme Court of Mongolia because the Mongolian Copper Corporation is a private corporation, not a state entity. In 2017, Bloomberg News Mongolia reported that Mongolia's parliament nationalized the mine assets by declaring the deal of four-hundred-million dollars illegal (Kohn 2017).

High-stakes mining deals and domineering foreign investment in handling mineral resources in an economy with a relatively uncertain legal environment enable political games and corruption. Corruption in mining in Mongolia is well known and the elites often leverage the mining licenses and privatization of state-owned socialist-era properties for political and economic gains. Several coal, copper, and iron mines like Bayanteeg, Mogoin Gol, Baganuur, Darkhan, and Erdenet have been state-owned mines since the 1960s and 1970s. The state has privatized many state-owned enterprises (SOE) in several phases since the 1990s, but still owns big mines like TT and Erdenet. The World Bank and mining sector reports point out the inefficiencies of SOE and call for better management. The remoteness, land-locked location, bad transportation infrastructure, and uncertain legal environment all require higher initial investment and caution, and at the same time, lure foreign and big multinationals. Mongolia's 1992 constitution recognizes private property and private ownership and only a few laws since then were adopted to address mining resources and related environmental and societal issues. They include amended and edited Laws on Minerals of 2010, Laws on Water of 2012, Laws on Investment of 2013 and the Law to Prohibit Mineral Exploitation and Mining Operations at Headwaters of Rivers, Protected Zones of Water Reservoirs and Forested Areas of 2013 (known as the long name law). Also, some tax laws and land laws have been amended and reedited.

According to the Law on Minerals of 2006, the state can own up to 34 percent of the shares in "strategically important mineral deposits," defined as deposits that can have a significant impact on the national security, economy, and social development, if the deposit is discovered by private funds, and up to 50 percent if it is determined by state funds (World Bank 2021). OT and TT, for instance, are defined as strategically important mineral deposits, and the government has 34 percent of OT shares and 85.2 percent of shares (more than the law allows) in TT, one of the world's largest coal deposits, conveniently located 240 kilometers from the Chinese border. Erdenes Mongol is a state-owned company that manages these natural resource deposits on behalf of the government. TT was two-thirds owned by Ivanhoe Mines until 2019 when the government purchased its shares.

Once the state is a shareholder, tax collector, and regulator in mining, it has internal conflicts of interest, eroding internal checks and balances as other countries' experiences show. Erdenes Mongols' case is not an exception. The company is a multi-asset state-owned enterprise in mining, mineral processing, oil and gas, transportation, border facilities, and engineering. The company did not report profits until 2016 and often gets bailed out by public banks like the Development Bank. The government initially purchased the shares of OT by borrowing from Rio Tinto via a London-based bank with 6.5 percent interest rate. In 2021, Erdenes Tavantolgoi company released a bond worth seven hundred million US dollars to raise money for developing a railway to China and a power plant facility for coal washing. 60 percent of Mongolia's coal is exported to China and the transportation of coal to China by trucks has caused environmental damage to herders in the region, which I will discuss below. Unpredictable coal prices and the Chinese government's focus on clean energy have presented challenges for raising money (Tumurtogoo 2021). The international bid to raise funds was canceled previously in 2011 due to unfairness complaints by Japan and Korea, two participants in the bid process (Jamasmie 2020).

Tax arbitration stalemates in OT and the annulment of international bids in TT taint foreign investors' confidence in Mongolian mines, and some investors derogatorily call the Mongolian government's desire for control of mines "resource nationalism" ("Before the Gold Rush" 2013). Even though many countries advocate for the local control of mines, SOE control of Erdenes Mongol is mired in patronage and corruption, and drains the public funds.

The Resource-Dependent Economy and National Debt

Responsible mining can theoretically contribute to the transition of a low- or middle-income resource-dependent country in the global south to a medium- or higher-income country, but so far, there is no single country that has made this transition. This is also known as the "resource curse" in developing countries that exacerbates economic and social maladies such as corruption, income disparity, environmental degradation, and social injustice.

Mongolia's case can be compared to other countries in the global south that are increasingly dependent on extractive industries, while developed countries move away from extractive and resource economies. The ICMM, which assesses the roles of mining in national economies and produces the MCI reports each year, ranks Mongolia third among 183 countries in 2020 and defines it as a "mining-dependent country." According to ICMM (2020), a country qualifies as a "mining dependent" or "natural resource dependent" country when metals and minerals account for more than 20 percent of exports by value and their mineral rents are more than 10 percent of the GDP.

Along with the analysis of the hyping of the mineral state rhetoric discussed above, in this section, I analyze the soaring direct investment into mining and the related increase in foreign debt in Mongolia. Figure 3.1 below shows how the external debt grew remarkably starting in 2009 when the OT contract was signed. As of 2020 the Mongolian external debt stood at 32.361-billion US dollars, which is more than 246 percent of the country's 13.14-billion US-dollar GDP ("Mongolia Indicators" 2020).

Big mining projects and related infrastructure require heavy foreign investment, and to raise the funds the Mongolian government issued several government bonds naming them Chinggis, Mazaalai, Gerege, Khuraldai and Nomad. It appeared that the Chinggis bond, for example, was a big success in 2012, building 1.5-billion US dollars with five- and ten-year terms and promissory notes yielding 4.125 and 5.125 percent respectively (Frangos and Natarajan 2012). At that time, the economic growth was 12 percent and foreign investors rushed to fund new-found mineral mines. However, when the bond terms matured, the projects were not realized, making it impossible to pay back the investment. In 2017, the IMF bailed out Mongolia for 5.5-billion dollars under the condition that Mongolia diversify its economy (Edwards 2017).

Concern over the foreign debt in itself is not the focus of this chapter since many mineral-rich developed nations like Australia, Canada, and the United

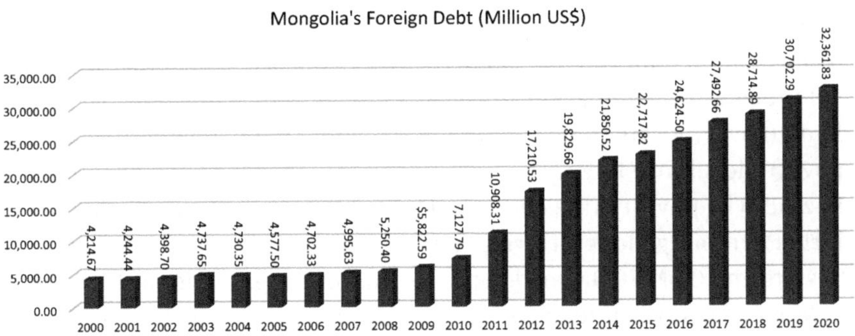

Figure 3.1. Foreign debt in million US dollars (2000–20) based on data retrieved from Bank of Mongolia

States carry a great amount of foreign debt that is equal to a multiple of their GDPs. In Mongolia, however, the benefits of mining-led economic growth are not sufficiently evident in terms of people's lives, while environmental degradation and the social impacts of mining are apparent. The government did not implement the projects promised in the bond, and neither did they formulate effective social plans that could have benefitted the country. The long-talked-about projects, such as improvements in the transportation of coal and copper to China by road and railway, have not yet started. The major border station to China Gashuun Sukhait, for example, still has lines of trucks transporting minerals to China, and this queue could be as long as one-hundred kilometers waiting to pass the border (NPR 2019). People in the province have their pastureland polluted by these trucks. Camels and other animals are hit and killed, and the drivers transporting them wait for hours and lose income. Politicians poorly negotiated the terms of the mining contracts, managed the revenues without a proper long-term strategy, and, even worse, spent the money raised with bonds on political gains and personal enrichment.

The tax avoidance by mining corporations and the volatility of mineral prices also exacerbated the above situation involving irresponsible government spending. The investment write-off by Rio Tinto for the underground development plan has been one of the major tensions between the two sides in the international arbitration courts because it reduces the tax revenue of Mongolia. Furthermore, uncontrollable factors such as the commodity price and the COVID-19 pandemic diminish the whole economy: the GDP growth of 17 percent reported in 2011 moved to 1–2 percent in 2016, and -5.3 percent in 2020 because of the pandemic.

The Mongolian government seems to lack a long-term strategy and the perseverance to transfer short-term mining investment and revenue into growth and poverty reduction projects. It is concerning that foreign debt reached more than 240 percent of the GDP while the percentage of people living below the national poverty level is staying at the same level. The World Bank (2021) reports that the number of people living below the national poverty level rose to 29.6 percent in 2016 and remained at 28.4 percent in 2018. The poverty rate decreased between 2011–4, partially due to the influx of mining money. During the socialist era in the 1980s, aid from the Soviets and COMECON made up one-third of the gross domestic product of Mongolia. Now, mines have replaced the dependency on Soviet aid at an even larger scale. The mining dependency has contributed to the increasing national debt.

The 2009 contract, on the development and exploitation of the OT (Turquoise Hill) copper and gold mine between Rio Tinto and Mongolia, makes clear the newness and weakness of Mongolian institutions which were not prepared legally or knowledgeably to negotiate with multinational corporations in renting mineral resources. Since 2009, a few environmental laws have been written or amended to address environmental degradation, unjust revenue distribution, and other societal issues of mining. These laws include 2012 Law on Water, 2009 Law to Prohibit Mineral Exploitation and Mining Operations at Headwaters of Rivers, Protected Zones of Water Reservoirs and Forested Areas, and the 2013 Law on Foreign Investment.

In the context of poor governance and weak institutions, an influx of big investments into mining contributes to increased foreign debt and heightened levels of financial mismanagement and corruption. Natural resources will run out, and environmental degradation will not be fully recovered—80 percent of Mongolia's land, especially the desert areas, is prone to climate change, and water resources are hard to recover. Even though new laws have been drafted to improve environmental conditions to international standards, and mining corporations like OT use efficient water rehabilitating systems, these standards are relatively new and are not fully enforced.

The environmental impact assessment is another rudimentary legal and practical area. The 2012 Law on Environmental Impact Assessment was amended several times with the "polluter pays" principle and often relies on industry self-regulation. When environmental and social consequences outweigh the benefits, the increase in foreign private investment in mining seems to be benefiting foreign corporations more than Mongolians. The question that still remains unanswered is: "Can the new-found wealth be spent on reducing resource dependency and poverty without falling into the 'resource curse' that has afflicted many developing countries?"

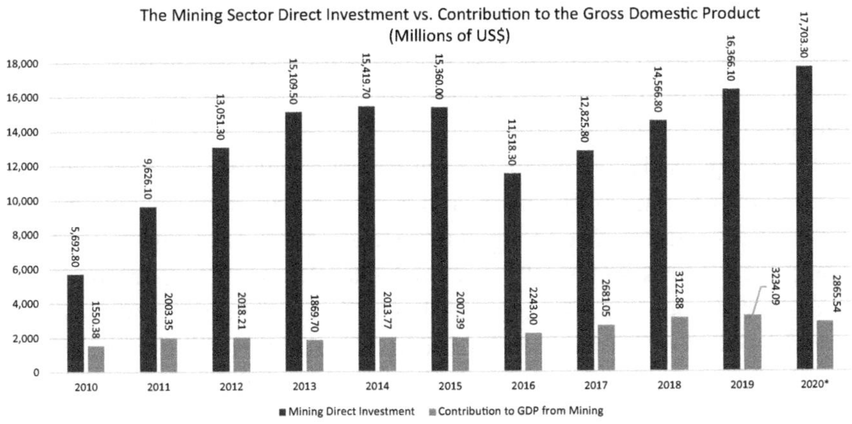

Figure 3.2. The mining sector's direct investment and GDP contribution amounts (in million US dollars). Data are retrieved from the National Statistics Office (NSO) website and converted to the US Dollars based on yearly average currency rates reported at https://www.exchangerates.org.uk/. Direct investment amounts in the US Dollars are obtained from Mongol Bank from http://stat.mongolbank.mn/?r=1112

To understand the confluences of the global capital flow and the local socioeconomic development, I resort to the analysis of the accumulation and distribution of wealth following Thomas Piketty's (2014) political economy analysis in his book *Capital in the Twenty-First Century.* He uses a ratio between capital investment and economic growth to argue that the rise of capital has enormously exceeded the economic growth over the years in capitalist countries. The ratio between the return on foreign investment and the income the Mongolian state receives from renting its land and minerals could be useful in analyzing the accumulation and distribution of wealth between the global capital and Mongolia's economic growth in terms of GDP.

Figure 3.2 above shows the economic indicators collated from the websites of the National Statistics Office (NSO), the Bank of Mongolia, the World Bank, tradingecononomics.com, and exchangerates.org.uk. It quickly reveals that, over the last ten years, the amount of direct investment to the mining sector was 3.67 to 8.08 times higher (or 367 percent to 808 percent higher) than the mining sector's contributions to Mongolia's GDP, showing the capital-intensive nature of mining which requires extensive amounts of capital from multinational corporations (NSO).

The figure above shows the direct investment amount and the sector's revenues to the GPD in millions of US dollars. The direct investment into mining ranged from 5.69-billion US dollars in 2010 to 17.7-billion US dollars in 2020, while the amount of dollars into the GDP fluctuated from 1.55-billion to 3.23-billion dollars. The dramatic increase in direct investment followed the signing of the 2009 contract between Rio Tinto and Mongolia concerning the exploration, investment, and exploitation of OT. These investments resulted in the double-digit growth of the GDP and tripled Mongolia's economy by 2017.

OT (Turquoise Hill) is one of the world's richest copper and gold deposits located in the south Gobi region, and it is estimated to have 424.2-billion dollars of resources. The Mongolian government holds 34 percent of the company's shares and Rio Tinto's Turquoise Hill owns 66 percent of the shares. The open-pit mining of OT began in 2011 and the underground exploitation started in 2022. It is expected that it will lead to an estimated five-hundred-thousand tons of copper per year at full capacity.

The OT contract of 2009 between Rio Tinto, Ivanhoe Mines, and Mongolia has been subject to numerous revisions, international arbitrations, and environmental contestations. One of the contested areas is the financing plan of OT's underground mining development and the reduction in investment from 15.52-billion dollars in 2015 to 11.52-billion dollars in 2016, while the mining sector's contribution to the national GDP increased from two-billion dollars in 2015 to 2.6-billion dollars in 2016 as shown in figure 3.1 above. Different circumstances factor into the ratios between investment and the portion to GDP by the mining sector. Mongolia's economy grew from 7.19-billion in 2010 to 15.1-billion in 2020, undoubtably because of the mining sector growth (World Bank 2021).

The data in figure 3.2 suggest that the role the mining sector plays in the economy has grown disproportionately in the last decade. I acknowledge the imprecision in translating currencies between US dollars and Mongolian tugriks by using the yearly average currency rates in the aggregating of the economic indicators accessed from these websites. In order to get a comparative perspective on mining benefits and consequences, I next compare the mining sector's investment and contributions to the GPD to the investment and economic contribution of the ICT sector in Mongolia.

Information Society Imagination

In an effort to discern how mining figures in the Mongolian economy in terms of direct investment and national debt, I compare the mining sector investment and economic contribution to the GDP to those of the information and communication sectors. The ICT sector shares with mining a similar capital-intensive characteristic requiring heavy foreign investment, and in this sense, similarly might add to the national debt of the country.

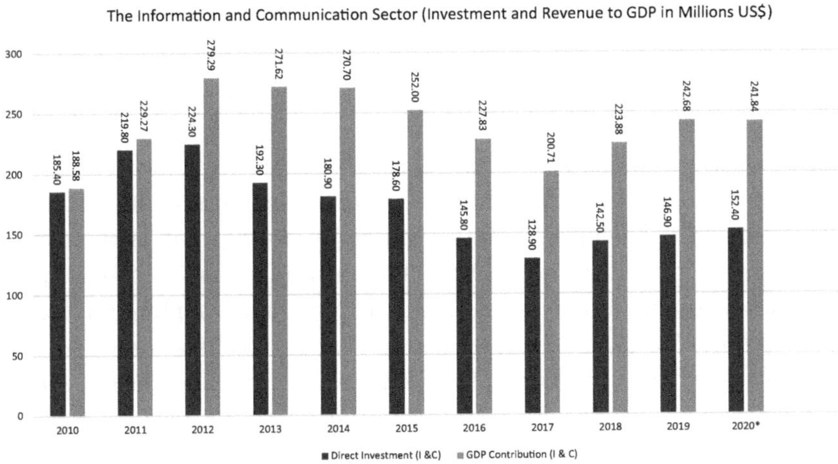

Figure 3.3. Direct investment and GDP contribution amounts (in million US dollars) of the ICT sector. Data are retrieved from the National Statistics Office (NSO) web site and converted to the US Dollars based on yearly average currency rates reported at https://www.exchangerates.org.uk/. Direct investment amounts in the US Dollars are obtained from Mongol Bank from http://stat.mongolbank.mn/?r=1112

The mineral-driven economic growth has led to increased access to mobile phones, computers, and the internet in Mongolia over the last twenty years and I described this development in chapter 1. The ICT sector grows with mining development partially as a supporting infrastructure, but with much less environmental damage and fewer clashes with agriculture. At first sight, the scales of the two sectors appear incomparable due to the much greater amounts of direct investment and the contributions to the GDP of the mining sector. However, this comparison illustrates the striking differences in the ratios between investment and the contributions to the GDP between the resource-dependent mining sector and the knowledge-driven ICT sector.

Figure 3.3 above shows direct investment, as well as the amount of contribution to GDP by the ICT sector from 2010 to 2020. In the last ten years, direct investment into the information and communication sector ranged from 128.9-million to 224.3-million US dollars, the lowest being in 2017 and the highest being in 2012. The contribution to the GDP by the sector started to catch up with direct investment starting in 2010 and the amount of contributions to the GDP ranged from 118.58- to 279.29-million US dollars. The contribution to the GDP exceeds the direct investment and the direct investments were the lowest when mining investment increased most in 2017.

If one compares figure 3.2 and figure 3.3, direct investments into the mining sector were 30 to 116 times more, showing the much-larger scale of the mining sector, while the US dollar amount of contributions to the GDP of the mining sector were only 8 to 12 times more than the contribution of the ICT sector.

These comparisons of the ratios between investment capital and the contribution to the GDP over ten years show interesting patterns of the economic aspects of media and information sectors in comparison to and in relations with the mining sector. Similar to mining, mobile phone and cable service providers including Mobicom, Mongolia's Telecom, Skytel, and Unitel brought foreign investment into Mongolia from Korea Telecom and Japanese Sumitomo as described in chapter 1. When mining investment was the highest and when the economy was booming, the ICT sector contribution to GDP was also the highest, the most clearly seen in the data of 2012. However, it appears that the investment into ICT infrastructure and human capital has more immediate returns and contributions to the economy than the enormous investment in mining, especially when it is borrowed with high interest.

Mongolian communication and information companies were created or restructured in the 1990s when the country went through the telecommunications privatization and liberalization programs following the collapse of the Soviet-style economy. This restructuring created competition and brought an influx of foreign capital. Foreign direct investment into the country should be carefully planned with long-term strategy taking into account adverse consequences. When foreign capital is poured into mining and communication infrastructure in developing countries it might create a developing economy indifferent to the needs of local people, even though short-term economic growth can be observed. That is why national programs and international standards with specific purposes and outcomes play important roles. In other words, who the lender is and whether a specific plan exists to implement projects for borrowed money are important factors for mitigating mismanagement and corruption in developing countries.

Strategies for direct investment are often created with input from home-country experts or epistemological groups. The professionals in the ICT sector in Mongolia created the ICT-Vision 2010 document at the end of the 1990s, which since then has been useful when utilizing donor support, foreign investment, and aid money as described in chapter 1. The internet connection of parliament, the online presence of the government, and rural internet centers were supported by the Open Society Foundations, the UNDP, the ADB, and the WB. These international organizations not only provide financial support but also transfer expertise, standards, and norms or at least work with the local professional groups to create an epistemic community in the ICT sector. This strategic document was adopted by parliament then and continues to be included in government strategic plans like the "Vision 2050" Long Term Development Policy (Vision-2050). The epistemological community in the mining sector, however, has not yet coalesced to provide strategic plans for the government.

The above analysis does not answer the ultimate question of whether or not informational acceleration helps people to gain the information and knowledge needed to find economic pathways out of the dependency on mining or whether informational acceleration is just one of the consequences or a necessary complementary infrastructure for global capital.

In recent years, a few Mongolian ICT startups, including financial and microlending technology company AndGlobal (https://and.global/), educational technology startup TomYo (https://tomyo.mn/), and open-source marketing platform Erxes (https://erxes.io) expanded their businesses from the Mongolian market to broader Asian markets. AndGlobal, for example, partnered with Japanese Marubeni Corporation to extend its services in the Philippines and Asia after implementing LendMn, a successful microlending, credit-scoring, and loan-dispersing program. TomYo's educational platform supports peer-to-peer education, study abroad, and language and other skills for its two-hundred-thousand users. Erxes.io provides business solutions for companies like Toyota, Xerox, and Godiva. These startups are often started and managed by Western-trained professionals, and while they need financial backing, they often conduct human-capital-based businesses with less environmental and social consequences than mining.

While it is too early to assess business outlooks, these startups make the ICT sector a possible diversification option for Mongolia that complements the mining economy. To achieve this desired economic diversification, the government should build national programs that channel short-term mining investment into longer-term sustainable human-centered sectors.

Environmental Degradation and Mining

Centuries-old pastureland cattle herding and the traditional nomadic lifestyle clash with big and artisanal mines and land excavation competing for scarce water resources, clean air, and pastureland, especially in the Gobi Desert. At the beginning of the twentieth century, for instance, the first Mongolian religious leader Bogd Khan refused to give a permit to Victor von Grot, a Belgian explorer who started the first foreign mining company, Mongol Or, to excavate gold. Bodg Khan's refusal was based on religious and cultural reasons against exploitation of the land. But his ruling was overwritten by the Qing dynasty emperor of China, which itself was struggling for its independence against the foreign states of Britain, Russia, and Denmark. The Belgian, French, and Swedish joint mining company Mongol Or was permitted to excavate gold in the northern part of Mongolia near the Selenge and Yoroo rivers between 1900 and 1920 in open-pit mines. It extracted around one-thousand kilograms of gold annually. At that time, only 20 percent of the mine outcomes were given to Mongolia and the mines were run and worked by Chinese and Russian laborers (MRPAM, n.d.).

Since the Mineral Law of 1997, mining capital inflow into Mongolia has resulted in environmental and social impacts. Reporters and scholars have documented environmental degradation and economic injustice due to the mining operations in Mongolia ("Mining in Mongolia" 2013; High 2017; NPR 2019). Dried-out rivers and lakes, air polluted by truck dust, pastureland pierced by mining tunnels, toxic dirt from mining also known as tailings, and displaced herders led to environmental and civic movements pressing the government and mining companies for socially responsible conduct. As mining interests clashed with cattle breeders in the countryside, citizens all over the country mobilized for their own livelihood. The Ongi River Movement (ORM) led by local herder Munkhbayar fought against hydraulic gold mines in the Ongi River basin since 1998, and contributed to the initiation of the Law to Prohibit Mineral Exploitation and Mining Operations at Headwaters of Rivers, Protected Zones of Water Reservoirs and Forested Areas and the revision of other laws on environmental protection. The government had to close over thirty destructive mines following the demands of the movement. Since then, the movement grew to the United Movement of Mongolian Rivers and Lakes (UMMRL), and Munkhbayar was awarded the Goldman Environmental Prize in 2007 ("Mongolian Court Orders Govt" 2011). The mining sector employs around 40,900 people (ICMM 2016) and uses 24,400 hectares or 10 percent of the land, but mining operations own two-thirds of the water wells in Mongolia, around twenty-four thousand out of thirty-six thousand wells.

Mining Influence on Media Markets

Media reflect and shape discourse about the economic benefits, and long-term environmental and societal consequences of mining. Media organizations both disseminate the mineral state imagination of the elite and the government, and at the same time, a few journalists attempt to produce investigative and critical reports into environmental degradation and social impacts of mining. Only a handful of environmental and investigative journalistic reports are produced about mining in Mongolia, and often they are produced in collaboration with international media organizations as with Lkhagva Erdene's involvement in the ICIJ's investigative reports about the Panama Papers and Munkhchimeg Davaasharav's reports with Reuters discussing the anticorruption agency's investigation into some politicians' involvement in the infamous Dubai contract.

One of the early infamous defamation arrests of journalists involving mining companies and the Mongolian government was reported by Reporters Without Borders in 2011.[2] Gantumur Uyanga of *Udriin Sonin* and her husband journalist Baviya Baatarkhuyag both criticized the then minister of environment and tourism Luimed Gansukh for purchasing a million-dollar house in Zaisan, a posh neighborhood in Ulaanbaatar, after the government signed a contract with Ivanhoe Mines, a Canadian mining giant. Police arrested both by force on libel charges even though both journalists were freed a few hours later. A lawsuit brought by the minister against Uyanga was dismissed by the Sükhbaatar district court in May 2011. Like the case of 2011, lawsuits are brought by powerful companies and government officials and these have been increasing in recent years. Globe International Center (2019) reports that almost 37.5 percent of defamation cases are brought by public figures, who often either own these big businesses or have commercial interests in them. Lawsuits and court costs involving mining companies have a large price tag that many newspapers cannot pay. This financial disparity between mining companies and media organizations pressures media companies to settle with mining companies and their owners. The audience of newspapers is small and it is difficult to spread information and create a financially viable model to conduct investigation unless international media pick up on the stories.

Investigative journalism requires a great deal of resources and commitment from media organizations; thus, only a few journalist pursue it in Mongolia. Journalists are poorly paid, and young journalists are frequently threatened by entrenched political and economic powers. There is an effort by a coalition of three daily newspapers *Unuuder, Udriin Media*, and *Zuunii Medee* to collaborate on investigative journalism and share the costs of travel expenses to mining sites. One of the interviewees from *Unuuder* newspaper

2 https://www.refworld.org/pdfid/4e37d4742.pdf; See also a Mongolian report at https://gogo.mn/r/ll599.

explains what an uphill battle the newspaper fought when it published a mining company story by stating:

> We once reported on a mining company in Govi-Altai province. The iron ore is close to the Chinese border, and at least ten heavy trucks parallelly drive across the pastureland, creating a great amount of dust pollution. When the mining company applied for a license, they promised to build a paved road. But they never fixed the road, and they totally discarded labor protection at the mine. There was also a foreigner death at the mining etc. that helped the story be picked up by an international newspaper. The mining company even inhumanely put the body into a duffle bag, when they sent the body ... When we broke the story, the mining company sued us for a large sum of money. (personal interview with Bayarmagnai May 10, 2022)

In this case of *Unuuder* newspaper, the manager Bayarmagnai proudly said that the newspaper never settled and never lost a defamation case brought against the newspaper thanks to thorough documentation. The shortage of investigative journalism in Mongolia is conditioned in general by ingrained cultural clientelism and corruption that burdens and harasses journalists, in addition to the low level of professional training (Baasanjav et al. 2024). The number of cases suing journalists for defamation has increased in recent years due to the law that placed the burden of proof on journalists rather than on a plaintiff. In this culture, journalists face the choice of either giving up professional standards or negotiating professional and journalistic standards.

The influence of mining on media content is also evident when looking into procurement and public announcements that media organizations publish in accordance with their "collaboration" contracts. For example, in January of 2022, the Ministry of Mining and Heavy Industry signed a "collaboration" contract worth 260 million MNT with thirteen media organizations including television networks TV9, Channel 25, Eagle, and C1, websites ikon.mn, zarig.mn, eguur.mn, itoim.mn, and daily newspaper *Udriin Sonin*. According to the contract, the selected media websites and television stations will disseminate information about the government and mining companies on their websites and on air, for which each gets twenty million tugriks from the ministry.[3] Journalists in Mongolia routinely criticize these infamous "collaboration contracts" and the nondisclosure agreement (NDA)

3 Accessed August 1, 2022, from https://www.newstv.mn/a/2116.

between government and media organizations. Yet, media organizations more often than not accept the NDA clause that makes them refrain from reporting any damaging or otherwise undesirable information about the government and the company. This way, through government contracts, the state and big mines funnel political money into the media. These contracts silence journalists, who are in fear of losing their jobs, and punish media organizations, which do not get government and business contracts.

Media institutions are economically and politically dependent on government contracts and shrinking advertising dollars as discussed in chapter 2. The media's watchdog responsibilities are dwindling, and they perform lapdog functions when they get "contracted" with disbursement money. Furthermore, the Mongolian government bought back shares in big mines like OT (34 percent of shares) and TT (85.2 percent of shares) from foreign companies and is operating mines that are ineffective in management, thus contributing to the national debt as I discussed above. This situation calls for rigorous watchdog media in monitoring and disclosing the abuse and appropriation of public land and natural resources; however, media organizations are "contracted," "dependent," or "state-owned," making investigative reports rare. According to the Press Institute of Mongolia (2022), 11 percent of media outlets are still owned by the government. Mining-related discourses in media spheres are dominated by the official information of the political and economic powers, and these discourses are narrated and polished by state-owned or "contracted" media.

In addition to government contracts, media organizations also have sponsors of programs that pressure them into indirect nondisclosure arrangements. In television, for example, it happens as media researcher and professor Unursaikan explains:

> There is no written non-disclosure agreement you can show to prove that it exists. Only a company that gives advertising to a television station wants you to retract unpleasant or inconvenient reports about the company. Companies say that if you don't retract that "fire incident" or "water incident" story, for example, we are retracting our ads. If they retract ads, television gets a financial loss. It happens like this ... Your salesperson comes to you before your evening news program and asks that you remove the story about that incident because we have ads from the company. (personal interview with Unursaikhan May 11, 2022)

News and advertising are intertangled in the inner working of television stations as Unursaikhan explains. It is impossible to provide evidence of this kind of NDA when you work for media organizations. This also shows how editorial decision of news organizations are compromised due to their financial dependency.

Mining money expands media markets during its boom and at the same time, erodes the media's economic and editorial independence. The Media Ownership Monitor (MOM)[4] project of the PIM finds that political control of media and the media's dependence on mining and big businesses make media subservient to entrenched political and economic interests by producing "paid-for-content" and "washed news." MOM found that twenty-nine out of thirty-nine media outlets they investigated had ties to politicians owning media. Because of the lack of sustainable and viable business models in media, politicians who own big businesses utilize media to shape public opinion in favor of political and economic interests. State-operated mining enterprises along with big privately owned mining businesses funnel public funding to politically-affiliated media to maintain the status quo.

Conclusion

This chapter explored how the dominance of extractive mining defines not only the Mongolian economy but also spills over into social relations and public discourse. The mining sector is the dominant sector in economic growth and foreign exports, as well as in increasing national debt and environmental damage. In social and media spheres, the discourse of the mineral state looms large, precluding other possible development routes for Mongolia. The imagination of an informational society has been drafted a few times by the country's elite. The first president Punsalmaa Ochirbat's gold and petroleum program of the 1990s was an initial mineral state discourse during a time of dire economic hardship following the collapse of the Soviet economy. This mineral state imagination started when the exploration and cadastral information of the Soviets became open to Mongolians and the public when Soviet control lessened. In this chapter, I question the effectiveness of mining in comparison to the ICT sector in terms of direct investment and the sectors' contributions to the GPD. While both sectors are similar in capital intensiveness and debt-financed growth, the direct investment into the mining sector grossly exceeded its contributions to the GDP. This becomes clear when compared to the relationship between direct investment and the contribution to the

4 https://mongolia.mom-gmr.org/en/findings/ownership/

GDP in the ICT sector which was significantly lower. Furthermore, this chapter explored the debt accumulation, environmental degradation, and societal influences of mining money on media and public discourse in Mongolia. I argued that the formation of a national epistemic group in the ICT sector in the late 1990s and the lack of such a group in the mining sector in Mongolia made a noticeable difference between the two sectors. The ICT epistemic group created an institutional structure for adopting international standards and norms, as well as coordinating donor aid and foreign investment. The mining sector expertise was mostly proprietary and secretive from the very beginning and did not mobilize the experts in the field to build an epistemic community. The mining sector's international social responsibility standards are still evolving, but it is plausible to argue that the Mongolian experts who could have been helpful in dealing and negotiating with big mines were not there from the beginning.

The above-discussed institutional deficiency, along with the decline in international aid by multilateral organizations like the WB, the IMF, and the ADB, have contributed to the increased national debt. The elites who either own mines or manage government shares in state-operated mines have created bonds and dubious loans that contributed to a large foreign debt. Societally, economic injustice and environmentally damaging practices in Mongolia are on the rise due to ingrained cultural clientelism and corruption. The checks and balances or the watchdog functions of media institutions are very limited because of media organizations' financial dependence on big political and economic interests, and government contracts. This financial and political dependence is silencing the media and the public. The silence spirals down to society without any mechanism to correct the discourse and fight corruption and clientelism.

Work Cited

Baasanjav, Undrah B., Poul E. Nielsen, and Munkhmandakh Myagmar. 2024. "Patronage Media in Post-Communist Mongolia." *Central European Journal of Communication* 17 (2(36)): 247–67. https://doi.org/10.51480/1899-5101.17.2(36).573.

"Before the Gold Rush." *The Economist*, Feb. 16, 2013. https://www.economist.com/asia/2013/02/16/before-the-gold-rush.

Bumochir, Dulam. 2018. "Generating Capitalism for Independence in Mongolia." *Central Asian Survey* 37 (3): 357–71. https://doi.org/10.1080/02634937.2018.1493429.

Cane, Isabel, Ashlee Schleger, Saleem Ali, et al. 2015. "Responsible Mining in Mongolia: Enhancing Positive Engagement." https://www.csrm.uq.edu.au/media/docs/1171/j003551-csrm-report-conceptweb-mr.pdf.

Edwards, Terrence. 2017. "IMF Approves $5.5 Billion Bailout Package for Mongolia." Reuters, May 25. https://www.yahoo.com/news/imf-approves-5-5-billion-030728321.html?fr=sycsrp_catchall.

Erdenejargal, E. 2020. "Erdenet Mining Corporation named as top taxpayer of 2019" Montsame, May 11, https://montsame.mn/en/read/225021

Frangos, Alex and Prabha Natarajan. 2012. "Mongolia Binges on Bond Bonanza." *Wall Street Journal*, Nov. 29. https://online.wsj.com/article/SB10001424127887324020804578147014152179412.html.

Globe International Center. 2019. "Media Freedom Report 2019." https://www.gic.mn/public/docs/freedom_report/media_freedom_report_2019_en.pdf

High, Mette M. 2017. *Fear and Fortune: Spirit Worlds and Emerging Economies in the Mongolian Gold Rush*. Cornell University Press. https://doi.org/10.7591/cornell/9781501707544.001.0001.

ICMM. 2016. *Role of Mining in National Economies*. 3rd ed. https://www.icmm.com/en-gb/news/2016/role-of-minining-in-national-economies.

———. 2020. *Role of Mining in National Economies*. 5th ed. https://www.icmm.com/en-gb/research/social-performance/mci-5-2020.

Jamasmie, Cecilia. 2020. "Mongolia Cancels Tavan Tolgoi's $1 Billion IPO Plan." Mining.com, April 28. https://www.mining.com/mongolia-cancels-tavan-tolgois-1bn-ipo-plan/.

Kohn, Michael. 2017. "Mongolian Parliament Votes to Nationalize Erdenet Copper Mine." Bloomberg, Feb. 10. https://www.bloomberg.com/news/articles/2017-02-10/mongolia-parliament-votes-to-nationalize-erdenet-copper-mine-izobd7q8#xj4y7vzkg.

Kwong, Emily. 2019. "Mongolia's Long Road to Mining Wealth." NPR, July 31. https://www.npr.org/2019/07/31/741798613/mongolias-long-road-to-mining-wealth.

Lkhagva, Erdene and Sergey Radchenko. 2016. "The Mysterious Sale of Mongolia's Erdenet Mine." *The Diplomat,* July 9. https://thediplomat.com/2016/07/the-mysterious-sale-of-mongolias-erdenet-mine/.

"Mining in Mongolia: Do the benefits outweigh the risks?" *BBC News*, March 12, 2013. https://www.bbc.com/news/av/business-21751072.

"Mongolia Indicators." Trading Economics, https://tradingeconomics.com/mongolia/indicators

"Mongolian Court Orders Govt to Enforce Mining Ban." *Reuters*, October 21, 2011. https://www.reuters.com/article/mongolia-mining-environment-idINL3E7LL05V20111021.

MRPAM. n.d. *Ашигт малтмал, газрын тосны газар*. Mrpam.gov.mn. https://mrpam.gov.mn/news/1326.

Munkhchimeg, Davaasharav and Barbara Lewis. 2019. "Mongolia lawmakers seek to rewrite Oyu Tolgoi deal." Mining.com, April 4. https://www.mining.com/web/mongolia-lawmakers-seek-rewrite-oyu-tolgoi-deal/.

Piketty, Thomas. 2014. *Capital in the Twenty-First Century.* Harvard University Press.

Tumurtogoo, Anand. 2021. "Seeking to unseat Australia, Mongolia's Giant Coal Mine Plans $700 Mln Bond." Reuters, April 21. https://www.reuters.com/article/mongolia-coal-idUSL4N2ME0MU.

Turquoise Hill Resources. 2021. "Turquoise Hill Provides an Update on the Tax Arbitration and Discussions with the Government of Mongolia and Proposed Class Action." US Securities and Exchange Commission, Jan. 11. https://www.sec.gov/Archives/edgar/data/1158041/000119312521005836/d217429dex991.htm.

"Vision-2050" Long-Term Development Plan of Mongolia. Annex 1 to resolution 52, 2020. https://cabinet.gov.mn/wp-content/uploads/2050_VISION_LONG-TERM-DEVELOPMENT-POLICY.pdf.

World Bank. 2020. "Mongolia." Accessed Jan 5 2022 https://data.worldbank.org/country/mongolia.

World Bank. 2021. *The Role of the State in Mongolia's Mining Sector.* https://openknowledge.worldbank.org/bitstream/handle/10986/37298/P173631074c-7de069090eb01f85e276b405.pdf?sequence=1&isAllowed=y.

4. Media Law and Regulation in a Digital Age

Abstract: The 1992 constitution and the 1998 Law on Media Freedom warranted the eradication of socialist-era censorship in overwhelming support of liberal and private media. The legal environment led to the mushrooming of newspapers in the late 1990s, along with television stations and cable service providers. Media laws left wide-open content regulations and competition rules among liberal media. The explosion of viral and interactive social media use among the public and the proliferation of various media and communication technologies create unprecedented challenges, as indicated by the increasing number of defamation cases.

Keywords: freedom of the press, investigative journalism, state secrecy, the public interest, defamation, privacy

Inspired by the new 1992 constitution, which proclaimed constitutional protection for free speech and freedom of the press, Mongolians who grew up in the postcommunist society are eager to express themselves on social media. However, they now find themselves constrained by the uncertainties of current laws and regulations and the inconsistent implementation of the laws by the authorities.

In the earlier years following the democratic revolution, the new parliament, The Great Khural, created media-related laws in the spirit of the new constitution, promulgating free and independent media, eradicating censorship, and mandating the dismantling of state media. The constitution alone was insufficient for dismantling the dominance of the long-existing Mongolian National Radio and Television and lacked enforcement mechanisms for transforming the state institutions. Civil society organizations led by the Globe International Center and the MFOS pressured the parliament to draft and pass two media laws—The Law on Media Freedom in 1998 and the Law on Public Service Radio and Television in 2005 (Baasanjav 2008).

Undrah Baasanjav, *Information Society and Media Development in Modern Mongolia*.
Taylor & Francis Group, 2025
DOI: 10.5117/9789463729888_CH04

The Law on Media Freedom prohibits the parliament from passing laws restricting media freedom and restrains the government from owning its mass media, and The Law on Public Service Radio and Television mandated the transition of state-owned national radio and television into a public service entity.

These laws were progressive in eradicating censorship in support of liberal and private media, leading to the mushrooming numbers of newspapers in the late 1990s and television stations and cable service providers in the 2000s. However, these earlier media laws left content regulations and competition rules governing the activities of new liberal newspapers and commercial television stations wide open. In the 1990s, no law regulated sensational and crude news in newspapers. This legal vacuum was felt once more when private television and cable channels proliferated, starting around 2006 when the mining boom brought an unprecedented amount of foreign investment into Mongolia. Programming requirements for commercial television stations were very relaxed without provisions for "societal obligations," and television stations barely followed the minimum programming guidelines until the 2019 Broadcasting Law. The new government agency that replaced the socialist-era government censorship authority, the Communication Regulatory Committee (CRC), has general technological expertise but does not have media and programming expertise. This situation backfired in Mongolian society, which saw the rise of politically affiliated television stations and a spiking number of defamation and libel cases in the media (Baasanvav 2016).

Recent increases in defamation cases on social media and elites' reactions to them by the criminalization of "obviously false information" during the COVID-19 years, as I discuss below, indicate uncertainties citizens and media organizations face regarding their free speech and the media's independence. The explosion of viral and interactive social media use among the public, and the proliferation of various media and communication technology create unprecedented challenges to Mongolian media laws and regulations. To address the challenges of digital and mobile development, in 2021 the parliament of Mongolia passed four laws related to public information access, data security, and individual privacy. These laws include the Law on Private Information Protection (a revision of the 1995 Law on Personal Secrecy), the Public Information Transparency Law, and a revision of the Electronic Signature Law. These laws, along with the newly drafted and passed law on cybersecurity of 2021, create a legal framework for the digital future, effective May 2022 (Tengis 2022).

In this chapter, I examine how the media-related legal concepts of free speech, media freedom, individual privacy rights, and rights to be free from surveillance intersect with the digital economy Mongolia has been striving to build in the last twenty years. Mobile banking, government services, and private businesses increasingly use digital technology and digital signatures, and these new and revised laws strive to delineate conflicting notions of free speech, surveillance, and privacy. I start the chapter by explaining the changes in the media landscape due to digital convergence and the proliferation of various media types and platforms. I strive to contextualize in the Mongolian context legal concepts such as freedom of speech, defamation, data privacy, surveillance, consent, and control of information that are often borrowed from the West. The chapter also examines the concept of the public interest in television and its possible applicability to the hybrid media systems in Mongolia. Then, I try to assess the effectiveness of the new batch of laws on speech-related controversies, defamation, and privacy rights.

Freedom of Speech, Media Freedom and Media Convergence

The constitution of 1992 and the Law on Media Freedom of 1998 guarantee freedom of speech and prohibit the parliament from passing any law restricting media freedom. The original intent behind these two laws was mainly the eradication of the censorship of the socialist media and the restriction of the power of the government. These laws were written in overwhelming support of liberal media and enabled the elite to advocate for no restriction on ownership and little regulation in private media businesses at the end of the twentieth century. This legal environment enabled "yellow newspapers" to mushroom in the 1990s (Munkhmandakh and Nielsen 2001; Nielsen 2009), and in the 2000s an unsustainable number of television stations sprang up (Baasanjav 2016).

The rapid convergence of social media with liberal newspapers in the 2010s contributed to an increased number of defamation cases in print and online environments. The unprecedented digital convergence challenged the Mongolian legal system because concepts such as freedom of the press, defamation and information privacy have not been sufficiently delineated in the legal system.

Laws on defamation, along with current practices of police and court handling of defamation cases brought against media organizations and journalists, hinder independent media and journalistic development in Mongolia. The Globe International Center surveyed three hundred journalists and discovered that one-third of them were questioned by police on libel charges in the years between May 2018 and April 2019 (Globe International

Center 2021). When faced with the unprecedented challenges of social media, politicians have the impulse to curb and control because they are also on the receiving end of social media disinformation and smearing. During the last few parliamentary and presidential elections, political parties and politicians skillfully used social media in political smearing and other online tactics against their political rivals. The Election Law of 2015 imposed stricter penalties on libel and insult against political candidates during elections, which led to the inclusion of defamation in the criminal code. Following Chinese and Russian regulatory frameworks, politicians have proposed draconian measures. In 2020, a new article was added to the criminal codes criminalizing the spread of misinformation and "obviously false information" (*илт худал мэдээлэл*) on social media of a damaging nature to the reputation of public figures. During the COVID pandemic, the Communication Regulatory Commission (CRC) and the police created a directive limiting access to information sites deemed by the authorities to spread pandemic-related falsehoods (Purevsuren 2020). Those deemed to have spread COVID-related false information were fined two-million tugriks (around seven-hundred US dollars). This article was adopted following the practices of some European countries that made digital platforms responsible for defamation and hate speech. In 2017, Germany passed the Network Enforcement Act (NetzDG), in which platforms are required to remove "manifestly unlawful content" within twenty-four hours under the penalty of criminal law. NetzDG was adopted to overcome the inefficiency of self-regulations of social media platforms; however, it has been opposed by many international civil society organizations (Heldt 2022). These developments show that the elite's commitment to the freedom of the press, speech, and individual thoughts dwindled once it was tested on social media.

Like in other countries, concerns surrounding the spread of misinformation and disinformation over social media have been felt by Mongolians, especially by political elites who rely upon social media in their campaigns. Throughout history, authorities have attempted to monitor or suppress rumors or the "spread of false information," as they are often shared by the voiceless "masses" or marginalized groups (Coast and Fox 2015; Scott 1990). In all political systems, including both socialism and liberal democracy, people dissent and tell their stories by sharing information in their communities. Seditious talk by recalcitrant priests and kulaks during the collectivization in earlier years of the Soviet Union, or the antebellum rumors in the US South about the proclamation of emancipation, all were considered rumors by peasants and Blacks collectively in their communities (Coast and Fox

2015). Similarly, when researching how Mongolians discuss politics and make sense of the rapid economic changes due to mining, economic austerity, and environmental degradation in their everyday lives, Rebecca Empson (2020) noticed that rumors played important roles in her interlocutors' lives on various topics ranging from the drying of the river Tuul to the spread of measles in Ulaanbaatar. Her interlocutors, who were educated women suspicious of politicians and the media, made sense of the politicians' decisions by connecting tidbits of information from various resources about politicians' motives and dealings.

Rumors and populism are internal discourse to liberal democracy. Social media posts headlined such as "гэнэ ээ" (#hearsay), "ичитлэнэ шарилаарай" ("share to shame"), or "попрох" (appeal to the base) have become common expressions on social media in Mongolia. People circulate rumors and unverified information in their communities to make sense of incomprehensible situations and negotiate against the dominant discourse. Laws and regulations to censor and suppress rumors have not succeeded in liberal democracies; instead, journalists and media organizations have some normative expectations to verify information and tell the truth to the public. If the media is trusted to do their professional work, the public's propensity to encounter propaganda and official narratives with rumors or counternarratives subside. However, counterintuitively, digital platforms that increased a plurality of different viewpoints, have also contributed to rapidly eroding trust in the media system.

Recent cases related to the spread of disinformation or "blatant lies" (*илт худал мэдээлэл*) and politicians' responses criminalizing the spread of falsehood seem to contradict Mongolia's constitution, which protects freedom of expression and the press. While the spread of dis/misinformation is a global challenge that has not been effectively addressed, Mongolian law and policymakers have clearly faltered. First, the terms related to misinformation, disinformation, internet defamation, or factual inaccuracies are not delineated in either the criminal codes or in the laws on misdemeanors. This omission or muddying has led to legal interpretations that leave room for practices benefitting lawmakers and public figures, as seen during the election year of 2020. These cases involving journalists and individuals posting on social media, especially during the elections, reveal uncertainties regarding the protection of media and free speech when public figures sue for libel, as was the case with investigative journalists Budragchaa and Lkhagva discussed in chapters 2 and 3.

Second, the parliament included the spread of falsehood on social media in article 13.14 of the criminal law, which used to be resolved according to the Law on Misdemeanors. This move is not a recommended practice internationally. The amended article 13.14 in the criminal code of 2020 states that a person who disseminates "false information injuring another person's character and professional reputation" will be fined MNT 450,001,300,000 (around US$157–456), will be subjected to 240–720 hours of community service, or will have travel privileges taken away for one–three months. In 2020, 590 charges were filed for distributing false information related to the COVID-19 pandemic, political libel, and other defamatory statements. In September 2020, the police added a new unit to fight against the distribution of "fake news" on social media. The police fined people around two-hundred-million tugriks in total. Because the libel article was moved from the laws on misdemeanors to the criminal code in 2020, the penalties in those incidents were inconsistently applied, either referring to the criminal code or the laws on misdemeanors. Even though the number of cases involving media was relatively low in 2020, the plaintiffs suing journalists and media were state entities and public figures charging them with a lower than "actual malice" threshold.

Third, this situation creates a "chilling effect" on journalists and media organizations, stifling dissent and political criticism against state organizations and public figures. The plaintiffs who brought the libel and defamation cases against journalists are frequently politicians, state officials, and government bodies, reports Globe International Center (2021). During the 2020 parliamentary election year, seventeen cases were reported of a malicious attempt on the reputation of public figures and entities (Purevsuren 2020). In 2020, state entities and high-ranking public figures brought 37.5 percent of 106 libel charge cases concerning social media disinformation against media and journalists. State entities and public figures need to be held to a higher threshold in showing the "actual malice" when they charge media and journalists who might be acting in the interest of society. This higher threshold for charging media should lighten "the chilling effect" on media.

In democratic countries with constitutional protection for the freedom of speech and the press, the state puts a higher threshold on the evidence sufficient to proceed with libel cases brought by public officials. In the United States, for example, for public figures to file a libel and defamation suit against a journalist, they have to prove "actual malice" by the journalist beyond misstatements or inaccuracies by a media organization. In the 1964 landmark decision *New York Times vs. Sullivan*, the United States Supreme Court ruled that *The New York Times* had First Amendment protection in publishing a one-page ad titled "Heed Their Rising Voices" run by the supporters of Martin Luther King, Jr. in criticizing the actions by the

Montgomery County police in Alabama during the student protest. There were inaccuracies and misstatements in the ad regarding the number of times Martin Luther King, Jr. was arrested and whether or not students were expelled for participating in the protest. The Supreme Court reversed the decisions of the Alabama court that awarded five-hundred-thousand dollars in damages to the police commissioner and two other Montgomery County clerks who brought the libel case against the *New York Times*. This landmark decision shows that the courts are willing to constrain public officials who sue for defamation because journalists criticize their public performances. Indispensable rights to free expression in democratic processes have routinely been contested even in old democracies over many court decisions, and libel and defamation laws restrict free speech and media reports to protect individual rights to a free trial, personal reputation, or control of one's own information.

Social media's popularity, technological affordances, and global outreach make them desirable for young people in Mongolia, and many believe in the inevitable benefits of social media and think that their personal information is irrelevant to Facebook because of their language differences (Baasanjav 2020). Legal concepts such as free speech, media freedom, whistleblowing, and private information are often adopted from Western countries and are relatively new in the Mongolian legal system. Social media platforms enable some public discussions and might facilitate some political expression, while they tend to amplify official narratives. These nuances are being unfolded for young Mongolians, yet it takes time. The media's regulatory framework and media literacy are both challenged by the fast-paced online and social media in economic and education systems as I discuss in the next section and following chapter.

Media Proliferation, Regulatory Convergence, and Ownership Opaqueness

As media convergence spreads globally, the Mongolian media spheres have also proliferated with all forms of digital content and programs. Most streaming services, including Netflix, HBO, Hulu, and Disney are available to Mongolians. As of 2021, almost one-third of Mongolians (995,472 users) watch cable television, another half million (527,033) receive satellite television, one-tenth of the rest (303,691) are connected to IPTV, and another 91,845 people have access to multidimensional digital services (Statistical Information Database, n.d.). In this increasingly converged media landscape, broadcasting, cable, online services, and mobile services have varying degrees of regulations for ownership transparency, service fees, and standards.

Convergence in delivery networks of various media content and the consolidation among media outlets also lead to the convergence in regulatory practices worldwide (McChesney 1999; Mueller 1999). In Mongolia, various media outlets have been developed, funded, and regulated differently. Television and radio, which used to be the party-state's propaganda apparatus during the socialist era have primarily been supported by the state with strict content regulation. Whereas private companies developed cable television services, IPTV, cellular services and satellite platforms and they have little state support and almost no content regulation. Cable and satellite television operators have been offering subscription service fees for hundreds of foreign and domestic channels and programs, including American Music Television (MTV), and National Basketball Association (NBA) games. Now, they distribute programs, including broadcast television programs, over IPTV and satellite services. Cable television and digital media are taxed, licensed, and regulated differently from broadcasters by the CRC, and this situation creates loopholes for new lobby groups.

In this hybrid media system of Mongolia, professional and interest groups started to lobby for laws and regulatory mechanisms that serve their narrow interests by taking advantage of separate and unequal regulations of various content creators, distributors, and broadcasters. Industry groups, like the Television Association, comprised mostly of television owners, lobby for laws like the 2019 Broadcasting Law that establishes the state broadcast fund collected from cable and multi-channel operators. In article 20 of the Broadcasting Law, the state establishes a broadcast development fund that requires cable and multichannel operators to pay fees to national broadcasters for distributing their programs. The Television Association oversees the distribution of this fund based on audience research, which is almost nonexistent. The law has no provisions concerning who conducts audience research, what standards are required for carrying the programs nationwide, and how the broadcast fund will be distributed. As a result, national broadcasters split up the funds among each other and a clear competitive selection process for the national broadcasters is not in place. The intention to create a national fund for television programs ended up with the outcome that the cable and multichannel operators passed on the fees to the unsuspecting public, many of whom are unaware of why their subscription fees have increased.

A couple of media experts I interviewed were critical of the current practices of implementing the law that passes on the fees to the viewers of cable and IP television. Media researcher and professor Unursaikhan explains how this bad policy became law by saying:

> Cable companies like Univision now added around 2,000 or 2,270 tugriks on their subscribers' bills, which is very wrong. They distribute free television content while they charge the subscribers around 40 thousand tugriks a month. They should pay one tugrik to one station and another to another television station ... based on the viewership. They have a technological possibility to monitor who is watching what. Instead, they decided not to split their income and passed those fees onto the viewers. They also have their lobby groups, and now the silent and captured audience pays double. That was one of the unfair lobby outcomes of the Broadcasting Law of 2019. (interview with Unursaikhan, May 11, 2022)

She goes on to say that in other countries like the United States and South Korea the government does not support the development of creative programs with state money. Instead, they create a fair and competitive market environment. The broadcast law left open the selection process of national broadcasters and regional zones for television markets while establishing low thresholds on commercial television's independence and program standards. Despite some new principles on program standards set by the law, interest groups have heavily lobbied to make the provisions on ownership disclosure and concentration of media favorable for them. The original draft of the 2010 Broadcasting Law, with the support of the Asia-Pacific Broadcasting Union and the Centre for Law and Democracy, was delayed by nine years. In the end, the current law was adopted, protecting the interest of influential media groups and increasing the payment burden on viewers and the public.

Another significant impediment to press freedom in Mongolian journalism is the opaqueness of media ownership of television stations, cable operators, and multipurpose digital media web services. In the past thirty years, politically affiliated and commercially unviable television stations and cable and satellite operators mushroomed despite the small media market of the country, eroding the principles of independent media and diminishing the societal functions of media. When commercial television converged with IPTV, cable, satellite, and online services, and started to webcast digitalized online and mobile platforms, the disclosure of ownership became even more muddied. Article 19 of the Broadcasting Law requires television operators to disclose their owner and holders of more than 5 percent of the shares; however, this disclosure does not apply to websites, cable, satellite, or IPTV operators equally. The societal functions and economic relations among media businesses have been inconsistently regulated in a piecemeal approach for relatively new commercial television, cable and satellite services, IPTV, and multichannel multipoint distribution services (MMDS). The ownership opaqueness shelters political partisanship and paid content on new digital media.

One of the major hybrid media challenges occurring in media laws and regulations in Mongolia is the collaboration of mobile operators with global social media platforms like Facebook. Starting in 2018, mobile phone operators Gmobile, Mobicom, and Skytel collaborated with Facebook's Free Basics project in making Facebook the portal on users' mobile phones to selected internet services, mainly to Facebook only. This Basic service, available to Mongolians due to the country's zero rating,[1] has been widely criticized for violating the "net neutrality" principle, surveilling users, and hurting news and journalism in developing countries. When essential telephone services in the countryside are packaged with Facebook Basic and Meta's Messenger app, people in rural areas neither have the option to opt-out nor to consent. Facebook's terms of services and privacy statements are being translated into Mongolian, but the default setting is that consent is granted to Facebook, as well as to other public and private entities. Facebook benefits from collecting and aggregating user data without restrictions from mostly worse-off and pre-paid plan users in rural Mongolia who do not have options other than consenting to the use of Facebook's terms of services due to the lack of infrastructural access to the internet, as well as due to high data charges of mobile phone operators (Zero Rating-Mongolia, n.d.). Facebook's monopoly and negative influences on media and information systems in many countries have been documented by scholars. Facebook siphons advertising dollars from local media that produce news, creates unhealthy media infra-structural dependency via programs like Facebook Free Basics, and amplifies disinformation that promotes polarized and sensational information (Pickard 2022). A glaring regulatory omission in the Mongolian legal system is that mobile phones are still regulated as a basic utility with very few regulations regarding their roles in the public discourse despite the ubiquitous Facebook content dissemination in collaboration with mobile operators. The space-colliding and time-shifting digital media in hybrid media systems change political communication locally and challenge media laws and regulations in Mongolia in an unprecedented way.

1 Facebook Zero offers stripped-down Facebook services in the countries of the global south without charging data fees from the users.

Public Interest Media, Public Broadcasting, and Government Interference

In recent years, movements to extend the notion of the public interest to the internet have emerged among academicians and civil society in response to the normalization of surveillance, commercialization, and monopolization of the internet by big technology companies like Google, Facebook, Microsoft, Alibaba, and Tencent (EFF 2020; Unterberger and Fuchs 2021). Earlier internet services like Wikipedia, discussion forums, and open-source code-sharing sites had many characteristics of public service media that increased access to information and the public sphere. The proponents of the public service internet want to rescue the internet from the commercialized and surveilled current situation to one with more servicing opportunities for the public by introducing the long-standing media governing principle of the public interest. The internet's public good, including information transparency and accessibility of information in rural areas, has been overtaken by extensive surveillance, privacy infringement, and distorted informational spheres.

The concept of public interest media, which has mainly been developed in broadcasting, is increasingly applied to the internet worldwide. The definition of the public interest varies widely from country to country, and it often evolves on the principles of diversity of views, locality, and accessibility. In democratic societies, broadcasting or public service media laws delineate the commercial interests of private media and the societal functions of media in informing the public. These laws often set minimum standards for content, programming practices, and serving the underserved, and require television stations to promote some public interest services in return for their use of the public airwaves. Starting in 1920 in Great Britain, the British Broadcasting Corporation (BBC) model has spread worldwide. Public broadcasting is supposed to be independent of the government; its content addresses common public issues, is accessible to all, and is paid for by the public.

In the Mongolian modern legislative and regulatory context, the Law on Public Service Radio and Television of 2005 and Broadcasting Law of 2019 primarily necessitate basic mandates for media to serve the interests of the public. The former one was adopted to transform the MNB into the newly formed public service media and legislated the responsibilities of public service media in the postcommunist era. The Law on Public Service Radio and Television has several forward-thinking provisions regarding the right to obtain information and the protection of sources by journalists, mostly thanks to the pressure from civil society institutions on the legislators.

Borrowed from the principles of European public broadcasters, the law establishes primary public service mandates. However, this often-praised law mandates public service obligations only upon MNB and does not require other commercial broadcasters to perform any public service obligations. The law neither guarantees the right to obtain information by media professionals in private media outlets nor provides legal shields for journalists to protect their sources. The latter one, the Law on Broadcasting was long awaited and only adopted in 2019 after being discussed for over ten years in the parliament.

The state broadcaster since the socialist era, MNB has a legacy nationwide network and has the biggest inherited audience, and that is why politicians are interested in retaining control over it. Even though the 2005 broadcasting law guarantees MNB's independence from the government, the politicians have exercised firm control of the organization through various tools, including the limitation of possible commercial funding options and the appointment of the board and executives. First, the law also strictly limits commercial ads to 2 percent of airtime, much lower than the proposed 20 percent. This limitation makes MNB dependent on government funding, which makes the editorial and programmatic independence of MNB practically impossible. When MNB management proposes additional possible funding sources practiced in other countries, including syndication and franchising of its programs, the parliamentarians, some of whom own private television stations, vehemently resist (Baasanjav 2016). Furthermore, the process of appointing the governing body of MNB, the National Council, is not clearly defined in the law, and this situation enables political interference in appointing the National Council of Public Radio and Television (DW Akademie 2014; Mendel 2010; Globe International Center 2015; Nielsen 2009). The National Council is heavily politicized and usually appoints the director general and key personnel in line with the party affiliations of the ruling party. In 2021–2, the chairman of the board was changed twice, and the general director of MNB was changed three times. When we interviewed the former chairperson of MNB, he jokingly said that "political influence trickles down—the ruling party selects a new director, and the director changes key personnel" (interview with Enkhmandal, May 11, 2022).[2] By leaving the public broadcaster financially dependent and by retaining the appointment power of the governing body, politicians have control over the MNB reminiscent of the socialist era. This financial and political control situation indicates how politicians conflate the fundamental media

2 Baasanjav et al. 2024

principle, "the public interest," with the interests of the ruling political factions and government interests.

The long-awaited Law on Broadcasting of 2019 still does not define the public interest principle, nor does it obligate commercial television stations to perform some services for the public. Because the Law on Broadcasting was delayed for about ten years while other attendant technology and services were established, the requirements of the law on programs and service standards, as well as on the provisions for extending public services, were outdated and were only limited to the definitions of multipurpose and multiplatform commercial media. Limited standards for public interest services are specified in article 23.5 relating to language captioning of foreign programs, Mongolian content development, children's and educational programs, and emergency information. These requirements are minimal, and the notion of the public interest is still made chiefly relevant to the public service broadcaster—MNB, but not other media service providers. When the principle of public interest is narrowly defined, and public interest programs are not mandated, the societal functions of media, such as a diversity of viewpoints, an emphasis on locality and universality, are not ensured. The voices of the people in the countryside and underserved social groups are not heard in the media. This hands-off approach equating societal roles of media to mere economic and business interests of new media is reminiscent of the liberal media practices of the 1990s.

The narrowly defined public service obligation for broadcasters and new multipurpose and multiplatform media contributes to poor content and an increasing number of defamatory and legal cases in media. Theoretically, the Law on Broadcasting was expected to set a fair competitive environment for different types of technology platforms and to require minimum public service obligations upon new media outlets and platforms. However, the law has been heavily lobbied by broadcasters and business groups with political power. Article 20 of the law still leaves the power to nominate the chairperson and regulators of the CRC to the prime minister, as was stated in the Communications Law of 2001. Via this personnel appointment, the government retains control of the CRC, the supposedly independent regulatory agency which issues and revokes broadcast licenses. This situation fails to guarantee the independence of the regulatory agency (Mendel 2010). This communication regulator protects state officials and government bodies who increasingly sue media and journalists for libel and defamation. Furthermore, the CRC is in charge of carrying out and spending state funds to support commercial broadcasters.

The discussion of the process of adopting and implementing the two media laws above shows that two notions influence the definition of the public interest in Mongolia: a) the notion of the public interest inherited from the socialist era, which conflates the public interest with the interests of the ruling political party and the government, and b) the laissez-faire notion of the public interest that advocates for the special interests of media business owners. Both notions skew or derail the media's independence in reporting state and business affairs in the public's interest.

When a digital hybridization in the media sphere occurred in the 2000s with an increased number of commercial television and cable operators, new owners of private commercial television and cable operators, who often were either politicians themselves or had strong ties with political parties, embraced the laissez-faire notion of the public interests. In other words, the path-dependent notion of the public interest of the socialist era remains ingrained in the legal system, along with the clientelist notion of the public interest to serve the narrow political and economic interests of the owners or the patrons of media organizations. Individual thoughts and human autonomy, underpinning tenets in the public interests, have further been constrained with online surveillance and other attendant technology like video cameras, geolocation devices, facial recognition software, and artificial intelligence. Below, I discuss how the surveillance afforded by new technology has become ubiquitous in the country and how a new patch of digital-transition laws the Mongolian Parliament adopted in 2022 tighten the control and surveillance. Alarmingly, the public interest notion is now yoked together with "national security" in the new laws.

State Secrecy, Surveillance, and Privacy Laws

The Mongolian Parliament's passing of a set of "digital-future" laws in 2022 under the "Vision 2050" toward "Digital Mongolia" marks a milestone in a legal environment that acknowledges the urgency of delineating the notions of free speech, state security, individual rights to know, and the right to privacy. Inspired by the constitution of 1992 and earlier media laws, Mongolians express their opinions freely on social media. In recent years, public communication on social media has been used as a pretext for politicians to adopt restrictive laws on public information disclosure and to impede the right to access information. Furthermore, as the transition to a market economy deepens and the mining boom and technological changes occur rapidly, the pursuit of individual wealth, financial freedom, and land and property ownership has increasingly become dependent upon the government's digital registration, information aggregation, and online information transparency. In this section, I argue that recent laws introduce concepts necessary for a digital economy, but at the same time, these new laws redact some advanced provisions regarding the rights to access information by media and the public in the previous laws and diminish existing protections for investigative journalists and their sources.

The Law on State and Official Secrets of 2016 expanded the classifications of state and "official secrecy" to various records of government organizations and legal entities that were not previously classified in the earlier version of the law, the Law on State Secrets of 2002. These broad secrecy classifications of "closed" or "restricted" information have deterred journalists from investigating wrongdoing by officials and businesses, such as corruption, tax evasion, and money laundering in mining, vaccine distribution, and judicial processes under national security or other "official secrecy clauses." These classifications allow public organizations to conceal controversial information and circumvent the provisions of the 2011 Law on Information Transparency and Right to Access Information (LITRI) that oblige government and public organizations to provide comprehensive information accessible to the general public (Baasanjav et al. 2024). Because of these classifications, journalists, media organizations, and potential individual whistleblowers have less access to public records that are necessary to inform the public about corruption, human rights abuses, and other wrongdoings of the state and public figures.

The most recent 2021 Law on Public Information Transparency, the revision of the 2016 law, introduces the process by which public information is sought and obtained and defines relatively new concepts such as personal information protection, consent, and notification upon disclosure of private information. This law aims to balance the informational transparency of public institutions on the one hand and the public's right to access information on the other by obliging a wide range of information about government institutions to be available to the public. The law demarcates open, closed, and restricted information, and the latter two "closed" and "restricted" classifications apply to previously open information. Even though the law defines these new concepts, this law reduces some advanced provisions regarding the rights to access information by media and the public in the previous law of 2011, LITRI. By deferring to the state and official secrecy laws in classifying "national security and the public interest" clauses, the 2021 law appears more restrictive of open information than the previous law. Civil society groups point out that only limited information could be made public under this law, especially in tandem with the Private Information Protection Law. The delicate balance between the right to privacy and the public good of information transparency is tilted in favor of privacy for public figures in these new laws. By reaffirming the extended definitions of "official" and "secret" information classifications of the State Secrecy Law, this new law to some extent undermines the right to get information by media, thus, diminishing the role of the media to expose corruption and misdeeds by politicians. The state and politicians use national security and corporate secrecy as an ignoble source to restrict media access and control people.

Constitutional protection of the right to know and the right to be free from undue search, seizure, and undue surveillance were inspired by the *Universal Declaration of Human Rights* (UDHR), which protects these rights as necessary conditions for a person's development. Privacy is a human right according to the United Nations' (1948) UDHR, which "recognizes the rights to freedom of expression (Article 19), to a fair trial (Article 10), and not to be subjected to arbitrary interference with ... privacy, family, home or correspondence" (Article 12). The Mongolian Constitution guarantees individual autonomy (*хувийн халдашгүй эрх*), dignity (*нэр төр*), and privacy (*хувийн нууцлал*) as inviolable individual rights. Article 16.17 of the constitution grants the right to seek and receive information except for classified state secrets and lawfully protected corporate and personal information. The cases of defamation and freedom of expression brought against media and journalists in recent years test the delicate balance between one's right to know and another's right to privacy. Constitutional article 17.1.2 tries to balance individual rights to information with individual responsibility not to interfere with another's privacy by stating that "The citizens of Mongolia shall ... respect the dignity, reputation, rights and legitimate interests of individuals" ("The Constitution of Mongolia" 1992). This article has been tested on social media when the public and media expose information for the public interest or share private and "protected" information. The constitution also declares that "No one shall be searched, arrested, detained, persecuted or restricted of liberty, except on grounds and procedures prescribed by law ... The privacy of citizens, their families, the confidentiality of correspondence and communication, and the inviolability of the home residence shall be protected by law" in article 16.13 ("The Constitution of Mongolia" 1992).

While state secrecy laws and security provisions have been amended to protect national security and data breaches of businesses, privacy laws protecting individual information have remained rudimentary until the laws on Private Information Protection, a revision of the 1995 Law on Personal Secrecy, was adopted in 2021. The outgoing 1995 Law on Personal Secrecy was only three-pages long and protected to a limited extent the confidentiality of an individual's communication, health information, personal property and assets, and family members' honor and reputation. People had limited protection against the government, businesses, and foreign agencies' intrusion into their financial, health, and sensitive information. In the 1995 Law on Personal Secrecy, privacy and the protection of personal information were not legislated within the context of freedom from arbitrary interference; instead, the law defined privacy narrowly and pejoratively as "personal secrets." Since the law was adopted in the earlier years of Mongolia's transition to democracy and a market economy, the notion of privacy benefitting society in terms of independent judgment was not elaborated. This previous version of the law did not clearly define what "obvious harms" to a person's legitimate interest, reputation, and honor were. The law provides almost no remedy, and that is why it is rarely invoked in practice (Melville and Erdenedalai 2020).

Mongolian laws have been inchoate in that concepts like consent and control of information about oneself have not been defined in previous laws. Government agencies revealed the personal information of the people exposed to COVID-19 at the beginning of the pandemic with impunity, and mobile phone operators required fingerprints to issue cell phone numbers. Facebook collects and aggregates personal data with little to no restrictions facilitated by the Facebook Free Basics project. There have been little to no tools or remedies for individuals to deflect government and business intrusions into their personal lives. Legal remedies for acquiring unlawfully and disclosing personal information without consent are only provided to a limited extent in the criminal code and the Law on Misdemeanors of 2017.

The new Law on Protection of Personal Dataof 2021 adopts the Western principles of privacy and personal information protection that stem from the tenets of human rights (Misheel 2021). In this sense, the new law of 2021 introduces a fundamentally different notion of privacy, emphasizing private thoughts and individual dignity. Legal scholars acknowledge that privacy is culturally and politically bound, and norms about acceptable levels of privacy vary from culture to culture (Cohen 2012). As a legal concept, privacy includes the notions of territory (such as trespassing or intrusion), the physical body (such as bodily searches or drug testing), information (such as individual data), and communication (such as computer hacking) (Baasanjav et al. 2019).

Information privacy in the United States is based on notions of "human dignity" to be found in both "the right to be let alone" and "the right to control information about oneself," elaborated by Justices Warren and Brandeis in 1890 as the foundation of privacy law (Warren and Brandeis 1890). The balance between the right to receive information and the privacy rights of another is often balanced in court cases. These legal cases establish legal precedents. In Mongolia's mixed legal system of civil and customary law, precedent legal cases do not bear any legal weight and are not followed in later judicial decisions. Judges apply laws, but their decisions are not a source of law. Even judicial decisions of the Supreme Court have no further effect on future legislation (Melville and Erdenedalai 2020). This ineffectualness of case laws in Mongolia makes it harder to address rapid technological development and social changes concerning privacy and personal information.

The new Law on Protection of Personal Data of 2021 requires an entity collecting and aggregating personal information to obtain consent in article 8 from individuals whose personal information the entity is collecting and aggregating. In article 18.2, the law imposes the following responsibilities upon the entity collecting information: a) to make clear the purpose of collection, b) to provide an option to opt out, and 3) to inform the owner of the personal information about the procedure used to determine the use of personal data for other purposes than that stated. The previous Law on Personal Secrecy of 1995 did not have provisions related to protecting personal information and biometric data because it was enacted before the internet arrived in Mongolia in 1996.

However, the Law on Protection of Personal Data of 2021 does not fully recognize nor anticipate the surveillance frontiers of multinational corporations like Facebook and TikTok. Even though the law introduces the relatively new concepts of consent, and the right to control one's own personal information, this law provides little to no protection against corporate and state surveillance in the increasingly global world. In this late stage of capitalism, states and multinational technology corporations like Facebook ubiquitously surveil people who use social media worldwide. Zuboff (2019), in her influential book *The Age of Surveillance Capitalism: The Right for Human Future at the New Frontier of Power*, defines and explains surveillance capitalism, in which corporate power for profit entangles with state power for securitization, both preying upon citizens who utilize digital technology. She warns us about the intricate nature of social media mechanisms that collect, aggregate, and sell personal information and their behavioral instrumentation. The social media features of softly nudging, tuning, and herding, are intricately woven tools for changing human behaviors. When essential telephone services in the countryside are packaged with Facebook Basic and Meta's Messenger app, people in rural areas in Mongolia have neither the option to opt out nor to consent. Facebook's terms of services and privacy statements are being translated into Mongolian, but the default setting is that consent is granted to Facebook, as well as to other public and private entities. Facebook's unhindered access to users' personal information and communication clashes with the newly adopted Law on Protection of Personal Data of 2021. The law requires consent from individuals and makes Facebook responsible for informing and disclosing the individual about the ways their private information will be used. Article 14 of the law prohibits the transfer of personal data to a foreign entity unless consent is obtained. Similar terms of services apply to other popular social media platforms like TikTok and Odnoklassniki.com that harvest personal information with the default consent of the users. As privacy scholar Gandy (1993) succinctly puts it, a Mongolian user is a "contract taker rather than a contract maker" (195) like any other consumer of Facebook, which has no social responsibility obligations and is "indifferent" to the needs of global users. People have to trade personal information for the privilege of using the platforms. Otherwise, they will be excluded from participating online.

The innately global nature of social media and social and legal differences in various countries complicate privacy protection and surveillance. Social media transverse territorial boundaries between local and global, as well as between private and public. The recent revival of the "right to be forgotten" and the ratification of General Data Protection Regulations (GDPR) in Europe indicate some pushback against the all-encompassing surveillance and commercialization of personal data by giant tech companies. These legislative changes are affecting other countries like the United States and China. In 2019, the video-sharing application TikTok was fined US$5.7 million for violating the Children's Online Privacy Protection Act by the US Federal Trade Commission for failing to obtain parental consent (Jia and Ruan 2020). TikTok is one of the most popular platforms among teenagers, and its parent company, Tencent, operates from China. These contestations show that the battle for protecting human online activities from data mining and data surveillance by multinational corporations might be similar in many countries, while legal delineation of privacy rights, protective boundaries, and community standards are of the utmost importance locally.

Conclusion

Individuals' fundamental rights to freedom of expression and privacy are increasingly intertwined with online life in the converged media space. Mongolian laws and regulations inadequately address online and offline speech-related controversies, defamation, and privacy incidents and the parliament has been catching up to address these issues. In the 1990s, the parliament left unaddressed libel and defamation cases in tabloid newspapers in support of commercial and liberal media, and this omission exacerbates online problems today. This situation allows lawmakers to not enforce the public interest and social responsibilities on private media. Furthermore, the lowered threshold for proving "actual harms" in defamation cases brought by public figures causes a chilling effect on media and journalists. The recent defamation cases involving journalists by politicians in Mongolia illustrate the tension between the right to privacy and the right to free expression. In the Mongolian legal environment, tensions exist between openness and privacy, "community standards," and an "individual's right to know." The boundaries of communication have been renegotiated over the years in many legal and court decisions to balance the public's right to know and individuals' rights to exercise their free speech and the media's responsibility to investigate the wrongdoings of public figures. The Law on a Personal Secrecy was overwritten only recently, in 2021, in the spirit of the Mongolian Constitution to defend against infringement upon individual rights.

Both the newness of the institutions and the legacy of the socialist legal system contribute to formulating new legal concepts in society. In a couple of the recent laws, the focus on tightened securitization by the government led to the overwriting of the progressive and forward-looking provisions previously gained in the 1992 constitution and the 1998 Law on Media Freedom seeking to provide information access to the public and the media. The elite's commitment to the constitution of 1992 is challenged by the new batch of digital-future laws of 2022. In these new laws, I argue, national security and state secrecy clauses are advanced rapidly, while laws that protect citizens' right to know and their informational privacy protection lag behind.

One disadvantage of the Mongolian legal system in this process is that it does not recognize precedent court rulings as a source for future laws. This appears to be a clear disadvantage when balancing rights in the fast-paced social media environment. Mongolians and young people increasingly use these platforms to express themselves, practice their rights, and report news, while state laws are criminalizing defamation and the distribution of misinformation. Common-law legal systems build media-related laws based on precedent cases as a source of law so that laws can improve. The lack of case laws in the Mongolian mixed legal system is a disadvantage when addressing rapidly developing personal information and speech-related legal issues online. This circumstance also led to the inconsistent implementation of laws by applying different fines and penalties in some defamation cases in 2020. This situation threatens the rule of law promulgated in the Mongolian Constitution and the public trust in the legal system.

The conflict between old and new laws and contradictions in new laws creates confusion, uncertainty, and self-censoring practices in media organizations. In addition to the conflicting codified laws and regulations, the judiciary and police practices threatening media and journalists with political pressure and high-cost defamation lawsuits create "chilling effects" on the media.

One of the most significant omissions in Mongolian law is the relationship between local laws and international "soft laws" that negotiate with multinational monopolies like Facebook and TikTok. The internet and digital media are innately global, and the sources of misinformation, defamation, and privacy infringement are regulated by "soft laws" and industry standards worldwide. Commercial digital platforms like Facebook are "radically indifferent" (Zuboff 2019) to people's social and cultural needs, especially those in developing countries. Criticized for facilitating media-incited offline violence and genocide in Myanmar and the Philippines (Stevenson 2018), a Facebook representative visited Mongolia in 2019 and started collaborating with local authorities to alleviate the spread of rampant dis/misinformation. Like other developing countries, Facebook's influence on the Mongolian media information system is double-edged, as Pickard (2022) explains. By providing Facebook's Free Basics services in the countryside, Facebook takes more advertising money from local media.

Work Cited

Baasanjav, Undrah B. 2008. "Mediated Political and Social Participation: Examining the Use of the Internet by Mongolian Government and Civil Society Institutions." *The Journal of Information Technology and Politics* 4 (3): 41–60.

———. 2016. "The Public Interest and Transition to Digital Television in Mongolia." *International Journal of Digital Television* 7 (1): 7–22.

———. 2020. "Social Media and Credibility: Civil Society Organizations in Mongolia." In *SMSociety'20: International Conference on Social Media and Society,* edited by Anatoliy Gruzd, Philip Mai, Raquel Recuero, Ángel Hernández-García, Chei Sian Lee, James Cook et al., 230–37. Association for Computing Machinery.

Baasanjav, Undrah, Jan Fernback, and Xiaoyan Pan. 2019. "A Critical Discourse Analysis of the Human Flesh Search Engine." *Media Asia* 46 (1–2): 18–34. https://doi.org/10.1080/01296612.2019.1626116.

Baasanjav, Undrah, Poul Nielsen, Munkhmandakh Myagmar. 2024. "Patronage Media in Post-Communist Mongolia." *Central European Journal of Communication* 17 (2(36)): 247–67.

Coast, David and Jo Fox. 2015. "Rumour and Politics." *History Compass* 13 (5): 222–34.

Cohen, Julie. 2012. *Configuring the Networked Self: Law, Code, and the Play of Everyday Practice.* Yale University.

DW Akademie. 2014. *Seizing Opportunities: For Free and Independent Media Worldwide.* https://akademie.dw.com/en/out-now-read-about-dw-akademies-activities-around-the-world/a-17784282.

EFF. 2020. *2020 Annual Report.* Accessed February 5, 2023. https://www.eff.org/files/annual-report/2020/index.html.

Empson, Rebecca M. 2020. *Subjective Lives and Economic Transformations in Mongolia: Life in the Gap.* UCL Press. https://doi.org/10.14324/111.9781787351462.

Gandy, Oscar. 1993. *The Panoptic Sort: A Political Economy of Personal Information.* Westview.

Globe International Center. 2015. *Media Freedom Report: 2012–2014.* Accessed 31 July, 2015. http://www.globeinter.org.mn/images/upld/Hevleliinerhcholoo2015english.pdf.

Globe International Center. 2021. *The Media Freedom Report 2020.* Accessed March 1, 2022. https://www.gic.mn/public/docs/freedom_report/media_freedom_report_2020_en.pdf.

Heldt, Amélie. 2022. "EU Digital Services Act: The White Hope of Intermediary Regulation." In *Digital Platform Regulation: Global Perspectives on Internet Governance*, edited by Terry Flew and Fiona Martin, 69–85. Palgrave Global Media Policy and Business. Palgrave Macmillan. https://doi.org/10.1007/978-3-030-95220-4_2.

Jia, Lianrui and Lotus Ruan. 2020. "Going Global: Comparing Chinese Mobile Applications' Data and User Privacy Governance at Home and Abroad." *Internet Policy Review* 9 (3). https://doi.org/10.14763/2020.3.1502.

"Law on Misdemeanors." [Зөрчлийн Тухай] 2017. https://legalinfo.mn/mn/detail/12695

McChesney, Robert. 1999. *Rich Media, Poor Democracy: Communication Politics in Dubious Times.* University of Illinois Press.

Misheel. 2021. "Legal Environment Has Been Created for E-Transition in Mongolia." *UB Post*, Jan 21. Accessed Sep 24, 2022. https://www.theubposts.com/a/12392.

Mueller, Milton. 1999. "Digital Convergence and Its Consequences." *Javnost – The Public* 6 (3): 11–27.

Melville, Chris, and Odkhuu Erdenedalai. 2020. *Mongolia—Data Protection Overview.* DataGuidance. https://www.dataguidance.com/notes/mongolia-data-protection-overview.

Mendel, Toby. 2010. *Report on Current Regulatory Issues and Needs in Mongolia.* http://www.law-democracy.org/wp-content/uploads/2010/07/10.01.Mongolia.Media-Situation.pdf.

Munkhmandakh, Myagmar and Poul E. Nielsen. 2001. "The Mongolian Media Landscape in Transition: A Cultural Clash between Global, National, Local and 'no Nomads' Media." *NordiCom Review: Nordic Research on Media and Communication* 22 (2).

Nielsen, Poul E. 2009. "Media in Post-Communist Mongolia: Challenges and Opportunities for the Democratic Process." *Nordicom Review* 30 (2): 19–33.

Press Institute of Mongolia (PIM). 2022. *Mongolian Media Today.* Ulaanbaatar: PIM.

Pickard, Victor. 2022. "Can Journalism Survive in the Age of Platform Monopolies? Confronting Facebook's Negative Externalities." In *Digital Platform Regulation: Global Perspectives on Internet Governance,* edited by Terry Flew and Fiona Martin, 69–85. Palgrave Macmillan. https://doi.org/10.1007/978-3-030-95220-4_2.

Purevsuren, B. 2020. *Илт худал мэдээллийг Эрүүгийн хуулиар зохицуулсан нь.* [Codifying "blatantly false information" in criminal laws] https://www.mglbar.mn/a/3764.

Scott, James C. 1990. *Domination and the Art of Resistance: Hidden Transcript.* Yale University Press.

Statistical Information Database. n.d. [*Статистикийн мэдээллийн нэгдсэн сан*]. https://www.1212.mn/tables.aspx?.

Stevenson, Alexandra. 2018. "Facebook Admits It Was Used to Incite Violence in Myanmar." *New York Times,* Nov 6. https://www.nytimes.com/2018/11/06/technology/myanmar-facebook.html.

Tengis, S. 2022. Монгол Улсын цахим хөгжлийн бодлого [Mongolia's Digital Development Policy]. https://gogo.mn/r/k847w.

"The Constitution of Mongolia." 1992. https://legalinfo.mn/en/edtl/16532180497951

UN General Assembly, Resolution 217A (III), "Universal Declaration of Human Rights," December 10, 1948, https://www.un.org/en/development/desa/population/migration/generalassembly/docs/globalcompact/A_RES_217(III).pdf

Unterberger, Klaus and Christian Fuchs. eds. 2021. *The Public Service Media and Public Service Internet Manifesto.* University of Westminster Press. https://library.oapen.org/handle/20.500.12657/50934.

Unurzul, M. 2019. "UN expert warns against setbacks in rule of law and shrinking space for civil society." Montsame, May 13. Retrieved July 15, 2021. https://montsame.mn/en/read/189244.

Warren Samuel D. and Louis Brandeis. 1890. "The Right to Privacy." *Harvard Law Review* 4 (5): 193–220.

Zero Rating-Mongolia. n.d. https://zerorating.wordpress.com/mongolia/.

Zuboff, Shoshana. 2019. *The Age of Surveillance Capitalism: The Fight for a Human Future at the New Frontier of Power.* New York: Public Affairs.

5. Civil Society and Young People's Media

Abstract: In this chapter, I discuss the role of civil society and the use of media by young people. The Mongolian public sphere is expanding, indicated by a few substantial investigative reports and the increasing impact of civil society organizations. Yet, these developments are shaped by political cynicism among the public and the limited economic resources of civil society organizations. By examining these developments in the praxis of not-for-profit organizations, I strive to contextualize the debates about the promises and pitfalls of the digital public sphere in Mongolia. At the end of the chapter, I discuss how politicians use pseudopolls to create a veneer of civic participation.

Keywords: civil society, investigative journalism, pseudopolls, techno-populism, digital pitfalls

The burgeoning number of civil society organizations and media outlets, and the increasing use of social media by the citizens, suggests that the Mongolian civic discourse is expanding due to new media development. Their practices are also shaped by structural deficiencies of limited resources and social contexts. I use excerpts from focus group interviews with civil society organization professionals and survey and interview data with students I conducted with other colleagues in the period of 2019–22. An increasing number of profit-seeking and enterprising organizations on social media, particularly on Facebook, misinform young people.

Civil Society, News Media, and Expansion of Civic Discourse

Civil society is not easily defined, especially in postcommunist societies like Mongolia, which went through drastic political and economic changes in a short period of time. Civil society, in a broader sense, is defined as a heterogeneous form of organizations, ad hoc associations, and various

Undrah Baasanjav, *Information Society and Media Development in Modern Mongolia.*
Taylor & Francis Group, 2025
DOI: 10.5117/9789463729888_CH05

information and value exchange systems that negotiate contracts and social relations between individuals and political and economic authority (Kaldor 2008; Keane 2003). In the Mongolian context, civil society is constituted of emerging Western-like institutions and socialist-era legacy associations of women, youth, elderly, trade unions, Red Cross, and professional groups that are adapting to the new system (Baasanjav 2008; Beck et al. 2007). Since the democratic revolution of 1990, Mongolia has seen a steady increase in civil society and nongovernmental organizations. Legacy civil society organizations (CSOs) have inherited established structures, buildings, and other resources they can lease or rent to reduce financial difficulties. In addition to these legacy and new associations, a swath of new gender-based, environmental, diasporic, and online-based interest groups have emerged, expanding civic discourse and information exchange. According to the ADB (2019), there are 17,634 registered civil society organizations, 80 percent of which operate in the capital. Many of them do not have routine daily community-based activities. Women, media, environmental, and educational organizations lead the chart of most active civil society organizations in Mongolia (ADB 2019; Beck et al. 2007).

CSOs in Mongolia have used digital and social media with sophistication for varying purposes. Journalists and civil society activists in Mongolia utilize Facebook Messenger and Facebook pages predominantly because "the whole of Mongolia is on Facebook," as one of the journalists who participated in focus group interviews in 2019 summarized. The Facebook Basic project has replaced basic telecommunications services in the countryside and cities so that "when you message someone on Facebook, the person always gets back to you one way or another," according to the journalist. In recent years, Facebook Messenger has diffused into Mongolian society, including the countryside, where traditional media and telecommunications services have historically been deficient. Many civic-oriented, professionally inclined, or identity-bound groups of Mongolians coexist on Facebook next to misinformation-spreading groups. Social media platforms like Facebook enable viral informational sharing, reaching out to many people and mobilizing them effectively. Media scholars call these enabling characteristics of technology "affordances." Connectivity, networking, and dialogical interactions are digital technology affordances that help to expand civic discourses (Bucher and Helmond 2017; Poell and van Dijck 2015).

Media organizations have taken advantage of the digital convergence indicated by the number of online websites, solid legal advocacy, and some noticeable investigative and entrepreneurial news development led by civil society groups online. The PIM (2022) estimates that there are 191 news websites among 486 media outlets in 2022. Media sites ikon.mn, gogo.mn, and zarig.mn compete for the attention of the local Mongolian audience with multinational giants like Google and Facebook. Advocacy efforts by Globe International Center, Open Society Forum, and umbrella civil society organizations were instrumental in the development and adoption of laws like the 2005 Law on Public Service Radio and Television, the 2011 Freedom of Information Law and Right to Know, and the 2019 Broadcasting Law, as I discussed in the previous chapter on media-related laws and regulations. Thanks to digital media convergence, the number of news websites has exploded, and these Mongolian-language websites are the most visited websites, along with Facebook, Google, and YouTube. In the survey of 240 students asking them about their five most frequently used social media platforms, 20 percent of respondents mentioned these Mongolian websites, along with Facebook, YouTube, and Google (Baasanjav et al. 2022).

Young journalists explore investigative and independent media models in the hybrid media landscape exemplified by journalists Bolortuya Chuluunbaatar of ikon.mn who exposed fraud in dispersing the small- and medium-sized enterprise (SME) fund between 2015 and 2018, Budragchaa of nuuts.mn and livetv.mn who reported the sexual abuse case in the girls' soccer team, and entrepreneurial journalists Duuya and Nora at the Nest Center (nestmongolia.org) who started the fact-checking network. In chapter 3, I discussed how investigative journalist Lkhagva Erdene of Mongol TV collaborated with the ICIJ on the Offshore Leaks Database in exposing the deals between the government and big mining companies OT and Erdenet. The initial exposé by Bolortuya reported that sixteen politicians and public officials received SME loans from the government fund, out of which nine politicians were indicted.[1] The SME funds scandal generated extensive public outrage on social media and created a political stir at a high level.

In 2019, journalist Budragchaa published high-profile investigative reports about the physical assault and sexual harassment of young girls on the national girls' soccer team that the National Soccer Federation covered up. He broke the story on Facebook Live while he worked as a journalist at the livetv.mn website. He documented the case thoroughly so that

1 "Одоогоор УИХ ын 16 гишүүн, 3 сайд, 1 дэд сайд ЖҮДХС аас зээл авсан нь тодорхой болоод байна" [Sixteen parliamentarians, three ministers and deputy ministers took loans from SMEF], accessed Nov 30, 2023 from https://ikon.mn/n/1fdw. The Mongolian government allocated some money to support small- and medium-sized enterprises (SME) with low-interest loans at 3 percent interest up to five years. The exposé by Bolortuya and her colleagues tracked down the companies that received low interest-rate loans to prominent politicians and members of the parliament and cabinet.

other Mongolian online websites reshared and reposted in a great number. However, Mongolian mainstream media did not pick up the story until *the Guardian*, the United Kingdom's daily newspaper, published FIFA's handling of the sexual harassment cases in women's teams around the world, which included the Mongolian case. Only then were Budragchaa's stories acknowledged in the mainstream media even though he was gaining public support to operate his own investigative journalism website nuuts.mn (Baasanjav et al. 2024). In 2022, Budragchaa broke another investigative report on the corruption and misappropriation of the public fund case by the principal of a joint Mongolian-Russian school in Ulaanbaatar. He documented how the principal of the school exchanged the school's soccer field for a three-bedroom apartment in her brother's name and paid the company 340-thousand American dollars a year from the school's budget. When the story broke on social media, she threatened the journalist and filed five defamation cases against him. Over the years, the principal of the prestigious Russian high school has built an influential network of parents, teachers, and alumni who work in police, judiciaries, and even in the parliament. All defamation cases against journalist Budragchaa were dropped because his report was sufficiently backed by facts and evidence. Some of them fended her criminal case off by dismissing it. When the defamation cases failed, the principal even tried to bribe the journalist (Baasanjav et al. 2024). He broke his stories online on a shoestring budget using Facebook and his website and started to use micropayments and crowdfunding to support his investigative journalism. His supporters donate mostly small amounts of money. In this case, Facebook's affordances of connectivity and networking enable him to break reports on a shoestring budget and engage other online sites to spread the news and stories.

Journalists see the benefits of collaborating with Facebook in the converged media landscape and often have a positive perception because people easily engage on it and information posted on social media drives traffic to media websites and sources. However, because of social media's mode of operation, shocking images and sensationalized information get plenty of attention and interactions, and unchecked information circulates for a long time (Galis and Neumayer 2016). In Mongolia, journalists' training, fact-checking, and thorough reporting have always been subpar; now, in the age of social media, media companies are even more inundated by the immediacy and availability of information. Even prominent media outlets such as Eagle TV or the online site gogo.mn circulate and amplify dis/misinformation because they only have a few journalists with low levels of training who do not have enough time to check stories. Under the institutional pressures of fast-paced news production, poorly trained journalists report sensationalized news, scoop up news from social media without checking, and mistranslate foreign resources. To help train journalists, young journalists Duuya and Nora started fact-checking services in the Mongolian language after they won a contract with Meta (formerly Facebook) to become a third-party fact-checking service provider on Meta's platforms, Facebook, Instagram, and Messenger. Their site, http://www.mfcc.mn, operates as a portal for everyone to submit suspected dis/misinformation on social media, and fact-checkers publish the evaluations of the misleading information that is circulating on social media to debunk and explain. This service has become very influential, especially during the COVID-19 pandemic, so the center's website has a special section dedicated to checking COVID-related misinformation. The socialist-era mindset and the lack of understanding of media, to some extent, dovetail into a group dynamic resembling "the hive mentality" (Zuboff 2019) on social media when encountering dis/misinformation.

The most remarkable benefit of the fact-checking center is that it collaborates with other international fact-checking sites and follows established journalistic and ethical norms. Mongolian journalists are often ill-equipped when it comes to fact-checking and discerning falsehood in stories, constructed images, and deepfake videos, and have no guidelines on whether to engage with lies or just to leave them. Nor do media institutions have policies and guidelines for journalists to check social media information or deal with hate speech and smear attacks that frequently happen during the elections. While there is little to no editorial policy and guidelines, journalists bear most of the burden and accept all the consequences of their reports. Traditional media's two- or three-tiered editorial checks with section editors and general editors checking stories are no longer practiced, especially on online sites and social media. That is why Duuya and Nora, both trained journalists who worked for prominent media organizations such as the Bloomberg franchise in Mongolia and the Poynter Institute, in their center strive to incubate self-sustaining journalism models. While they started modestly by opening a Facebook page at the beginning of the COVID-19 pandemic, their fact-checking project has been relatively successful because Facebook pays for journalistic work, as Duuya and Nora acknowledged in a personal interview (Baasanjav et al. 2024).

In other words, Facebook's immediacy tends to amplify institutional deficiencies and professional missteps. Yet, compared to local media organizations, collaboration with Facebook is beneficial for journalists because, in addition to providing guidelines, Facebook pays for the work without being involved in their routines. Journalist Duuya initiated a similar project and was even awarded a grant from the Google News Initiative when she worked in a Mongolian newspaper prior to establishing the center. She felt she could not implement what she proposed because the newspaper was owned by a local bank group, which neither cared for nor understood journalism.[2] So it is understandable that journalists hold technologically utopian views of the inevitable benefits of social media, while having little understanding of either their embedded "algorithmic biases" (Woolley and Howard 2016) or "shadow texts" (Zuboff 2019, 186). Facebook's limited financial support to fact-checking startups, which subscribe to its fact-checking services and adopt its guidelines, are more for deflective moves when responding to criticism than healthy support for sustainable media companies. Yet, Facebook's external influences on local journalism have been criticized in other countries because the company siphons off advertising dollars from the local media it purportedly supports and creates infrastructural dependency with its Facebook Basic (Pickard 2022). Some of this collaboration between news organizations and Facebook happened following the collaboration visit by Facebook to Mongolia in 2019 at the request of the local authorities, as I discussed in chapter 2. However, Facebook's collaboration with the local authorities to alleviate disinformation and misinformation on social media has not supported civil society (Misheel 2019).

Women's organizations have been at the forefront of online civic discourse and participation expansion of civil society resembling their offline trailblazer traditions in Mongolia. Facebook groups like Women for Change and MommyCentral effectively mobilize and organize marches protesting sexual harassment and violence against children. These loosely structured, gender-based, and child rights organizations effectively mobilize their base and advocate for them in developing and adopting the Laws to Combat Domestic Violence of 2016 and the Law on Child Protection of 2016. Women for Change is a not-for-profit organization, which initially started in 2010 as a Facebook group of sixteen women discussing gender inequality. A year later, the group became a not-for-profit organization, the goals of which are to promote gender equality and human rights and to fight against sexual assaults and harassment including domestic violence. The organization coordinates mostly on Facebook, and the group page has sixty-six thousand members comprised mostly of students. The popularity of the group on social media even compelled the minister of education to sit down with them to discuss sexual harassment issues amidst the minister's denial of sexual harassment in Mongolian universities. Anu, a gender equality activist says:

2 Interview with Duuya, May 14, 2022

> We picket and march sometimes; but in Mongolia when the outside temperature is –20 Celsius and the risk of the muddling and hijacking protests by undue influences is high, media campaigns on social media go a long way for us. When we organize a street march sometimes people unduly suspect that the agendas of foreign influences or the Democratic or the People's parties are being played out. Young people in Mongolia struggle to organize a non-partisan march or protest. We post and boost gender equality information, infographics and videos to educate, empower and engage young women and young people. With the decline of people's engagement on Facebook starting 2012–13, it is getting harder to get and keep people's attention for human rights information. We adapt to our members' needs, but also try *not* to trivialize human rights issues ... We use Facebook for announcing and coordinating mostly, but we use books, journals, and other reliable sources to prepare our information and educational materials. (Anu, personal communication, July 4, 2019)

Anu speaks to the tactical swarming possibilities on Facebook when organizing and mobilizing an event and responding quickly during the event. However, she acknowledges how Facebook is not always the best place for explaining complex human rights and gender equality issues. She is conflicted when creating somewhat quickly "consumable" content for the audience which might cater toward the "trivialization" of complex issues. The embedded logic of social media promoting virality and publicity limits Anu's group from trying to sustain credible and reliable information, as well as sustain people's engagement. Political discourse scholars who study social media argue that people increasingly post safe political content in order not to be attacked or called out. A "context collapse" (boyd 2010), which occurs when an active audience differs from the "imagined audience" on social media, has contributed to the reasons why people do not engage deeply on Facebook (Galis and Neumayer 2016; Richez et al. 2020), and the engagement on Facebook has in fact been diminishing in Mongolia.

MommyCentral is another group, which was started by five concerned mothers who organized a march protesting violence against children. Journalist Nara, who observed the march, said that "the group [MommyCentral] was incredibly effective in monitoring the march and preventing the protest from going awry during the protest against child abuse and rape in March 2018." Some protestors among four-hundred-thousand participants demanded capital punishment for sex offenders, and the issue of capital punishment was thrown into the mix of the protest while most protestors were against capital punishment (Davaasharav and Bittner 2018). The agile reaction of the MommyCentral group on Facebook was very effective, and they stayed focused on the main course of protests without being diverted. These cases speak to the communicative and mobile networking affordances of social networks in "tactical swarming" (Rheingold 2000) explored in previous studies (Galis and Neumayer 2016; Richez et al. 2020).

Social media adds a layer to social stratification and exacerbates the divide between the capital city and the countryside, as well as between users of different platforms and skill levels. Educational and cultural organizations in the countryside and the outskirts of cities do not enjoy the same access and inclusive possibilities. Tungaa, a director of an educational not-for-profit umbrella organization, says her organization mostly conducts its routine tasks via email because internet access at its six branches in the countryside and two outskirts of Ulaanbaatar is very limited. They send documents via email and then check by phone to make sure the documents arrived. Then the associates in the countryside go to internet cafes and read the documents and respond back. Tungaa goes on to say:

> Facebook is very useful for routine organizational tasks, but obviously, we do not use it for the exchange of official documents. Yet, on Facebook, I really feel the popular mood like chauvinism against ethnic minorities and women. I have seen how Twitter users look down upon Facebook users saying that "poor, uneducated, dark mass" on Facebook discussing this or that ... I personally use Twitter for getting news, but I do not post much because attacks on Twitter can be very crude. We do not have a website because creating and maintaining it requires a skilled person. (interview with Tungaa July 3, 2019)

Tungaa refers to the necessity of visibility on various platforms and the differences in people's engagement with them. There is a perceived hierarchy in terms of platforms, in which Facebook is seen as more engaging, but has a broader "mass" base, whereas Twitter is seen as having a more professional or selective base. This notion of the small number of active users who post often on Twitter (now X) and its users' somewhat fragmented experiences go along with the findings of previous studies in other countries (Arceneaux and Dinu 2018; Matuszewski and Szabó 2019). Internet scholars have long documented the internet's tendency to amplify existing social gaps and stratification (Agre 2002; Norris 2001).

Environmental not-for-profit organizations have grown to become "the loudest voice against environmental pollution" in Mongolia (ADB 2019). They created an environmental alliance of community-based organizations in mining towns that fight for their rights by pressuring mining companies and the government to comply with international standards. However, local community-based organizations lack the funding to gain visibility and to build trained staff. According to the ADB (2019), 59.5 percent of the funding of civil society organizations in Mongolia is provided by international organizations, and they often lack the resources to get media attention. The media do not pay attention to important environmental issues because they do not get paid, and this situation makes activists bait journalists with sensational news, a well-known activist tactic in other countries (see Galis and Neumayer 2016; Gitlin 1980). Erdene, who works in an environmental organization, explains the dynamic of getting media attention for environmental issues by resorting to sensationalized news about environmental deterioration:

> Since the beginning of the mining boom, all levels of heavy metal and gas pollution have surpassed acceptable standards in Ulaanbaatar as well as in the countryside. Many people became ninja-miners (illegal gold miners) ... and they have no understanding of how much metal and gas pollution they bring in when they bring in one gram of gold. The mercury pollution at *Urt Tsagaan* (a well-known silversmith place in Ulaanbaatar) is 10, 20 times higher than the acceptable level. We used to post this environmental information and raw data on our websites; however, we realized that 1) not many people read our website, and 2) we got hacked and lost a lot of data ... So, we opted for traditional information dissemination and learned that journalists bite the bait of sensationalism. Journalists do not pay attention or come to us unless the information is sensational ... And then government organizations attack us for churning the public with sensationalism. (interview with Erdene July 5, 2019)

Environmentalists appropriate online and social media and craftily negotiate the online visibility for the public, and "invisibility" to the authorities when making environmental degradation information available (see other country's experiences in Galis and Neumayer 2016; Lokot 2020; Richez et al. 2020). The work of maintaining online visibility by these resource-poor organizations by creating counternarratives and managing the mundane tasks of protecting against hacking should not be overlooked.

Media, women, and environmental civil society organizations are skillfully expanding civic discourse offline and online, but they experience access exclusion, financial stratification, and institutional path dependency in their routine operations. While legalistically, the context in Mongolia is conducive to civil society and civic discourse development, historically formed constraints deter the expansion of civil society by those involved. In the section below, we will discuss how the new generation makes sense of new and online information and media development.

Young People's Digital Media Repertoire

In 2019, the average age of Mongolians was 27 (ADB 2019), and this relatively young population is drawn to visual, hyperlinked, and interactive information on social media on platforms like Facebook, which accounts for 65–70 percent of online activity (GlobalStats 2019). However, research exploring how cognizant Mongolian youth are of the benefits and pitfalls of digital media in their social and political participation is rare. Here I summarize some of the preliminary findings of the study of students' perceptions of social media, misinformation, privacy, and the appropriateness of media content. I conducted this research along with colleagues at the National University of Mongolia in 2022 based on some of the results of a self-reported survey of 240 students and qualitative in-depth interviews with ten participants.[3]

Mongolian youth primarily use social media for communicating, entertaining, and learning. When we surveyed college students in Ulaanbaatar, the result showed that students use social media most commonly "to communicate and chat" (192 respondents or 80 percent of the sample) and "to get entertained" (190 respondents or 79.2 percent), while the numbers of students using it for class-related purposes (153 respondents or 63.7 percent) and for the purposes of learning and discovering (169 respondents or 70.4 percent) have increased, as shown in the figure below.

Figure 5.1 shows that young people use social media mostly for personal gratification through entertainment, discovery, and social connectivity, using features like the chat function in Facebook Messenger. The pattern of predominantly individual, apolitical, or leisurely use by Mongolian youth is similar to the use by youth in other countries (Arceneaux and Dinu 2018; Ofcom 2021). The respondents in the survey infrequently selected the purpose "to get informed (news)" (59.17 percent), and the least-likely selected

3 Baasanjav et al., July, 2022, "Digital Repertoire of Young Mongolian People and Transcultural Implications," paper presented to the IAMCR 2022 pre-conference, "Digital Governance and Transcultural Communications," available at https://xwcb.bnu.edu.cn/sn/ln/132189.html. The paper discusses the results of the survey ($N = 240$ students) and qualitative in-depth interviews with ten students who creatively and extensively use digital media.

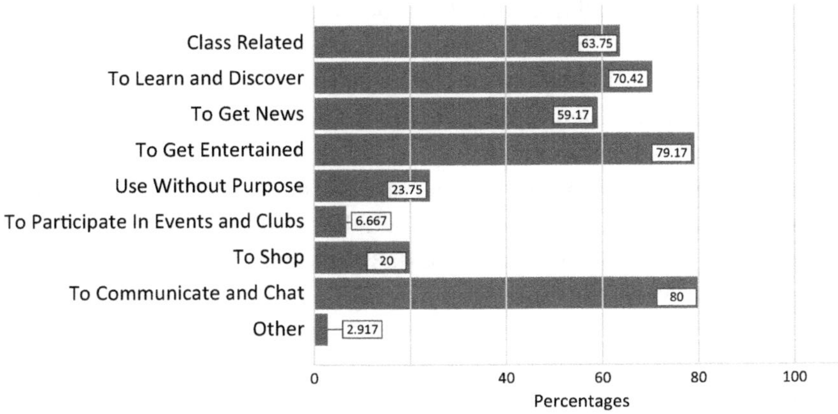

Figure 5.1. Common social media use purposes of students

option was "to participate in politics, events and clubs" (6.67 percent), suggesting that students, in general, seek out communication and entertainment more often than news and participation opportunities. Especially during the COVID-19 pandemic, when most classes were transformed into online modes of learning, youth's use of social as well as traditional media increased. During the COVID-19 pandemic, the boundaries of information, entertainment, and education blurred, and students unprecedentedly meshed learning with entertainment and news with other media content production.

In terms of social media platforms, global megaconglomerates topped the list—Facebook leading (222 respondents or 92.4 percent), followed by Instagram (216 respondents or 90 percent), and YouTube (170 respondents or 70.8 percent)—when we asked the students to name the five primarily used social media platforms.[4] As transnational social media platforms like Facebook enable local-language media content and local accounts, they predominate young people's virtual hangout places, blurring the boundaries between global and local, as was reported in global internet traffic reports by GlobalStats (2019). Notwithstanding, the youth listed Mongolian news websites such as ikon.mn and gogo.mn in the top five social media, mostly the fourth- and fifth-commonly used platforms (51 participants or 20.8 percent of the sample). These numbers indicate that the respondents surveyed either did not have a clear differentiation between social media platforms, websites, search engines, and applications, or they were eager to include local-language websites in the list

4 Baasanjav et.al. (2022) asked students to list the five most frequently used social media.

of frequently used social media. This social media literacy involving an understanding of social media will be discussed below when I discuss young people's media literacy. At the same time, the tide of online news media that mushroomed in the 2010s gets some attention from the local youth in their daily news diets.

Surprisingly, contrary to the expectations that young people post and share constantly, the survey results show a lower level of sharing, posting, and commenting in general by the youth. Of the respondents, 76.96 percent reported they "Never" or "Rarely" share information on social media, while only 9.38 percent reported that they "Always" or "Frequently" posted, shared, or commented. Furthermore, 22.77 percent of the students reported they "Sometimes" shared or posted. The students rarely share or post on Facebook because many family members, school teachers, and administrators are on it, creating a "context collapse" (boyd 2010) of communication among peers, family members, and school administrations. In the Mongolian context, most interactions occur on Facebook and the media-competent youth are aware of the pitfalls of the platform. They foresee pitfalls in sharing and posting when teachers, parents, and potential employers are all on Facebook, and many young people are even fleeing Facebook for other platforms for personal expression. Facebook Basic has been packaged with basic telephone services in Mongolia, increasing its user base, and Meta's Messenger app is replacing basic telecommunications services in the countryside. College junior Mugi explains how her work requires Facebook, while it does not gratify her needs by saying:

> For me personally, Facebook does not give useful information … I develop the Facebook and Instagram accounts for my job at the University Press. I create book-related content and create infographics for professors and students. Then, I schedule and post 1–2 posts on Instagram weekly or so. Instagram at least has filters that do not fill up my feed like Facebook. (Interview with Mugi, May 25, 2022)

Facebook does not gratify the interviewee Mugi's personal needs, but she utilizes it for work for the university publisher, which promotes book-related information. Facebook pages created by organizations or individuals, from police to university publishers, are often used as news sources by students (67.2 percent of respondents). More often, students check the official social media accounts of news organizations (81.5 percent of the respondents) rather than Facebook pages. We then explored why students share information and what purposes their sharing, posting, and commenting on social media

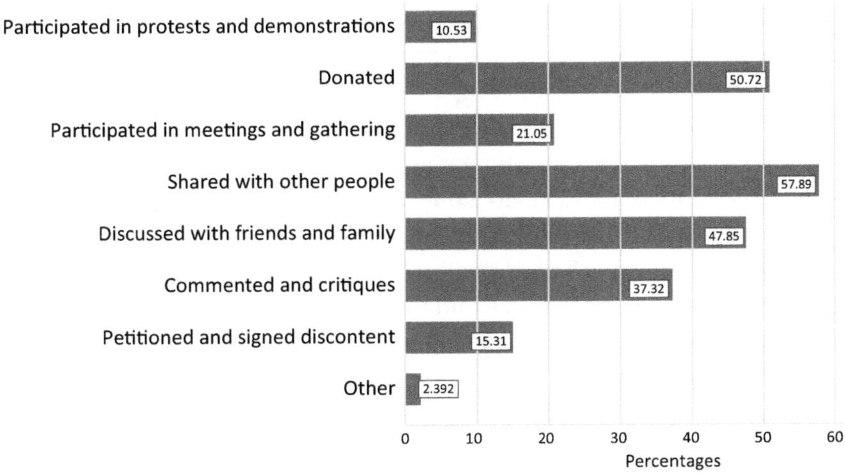

Figure 5.2. Actions taken by students invoked by information on social media

serve. Not surprisingly, 69 percent of the participants use social media "to voice and express an opinion," followed by 57.36 percent of "supporting others." Self-expression and supporting others are more prevalent than "civic participation" (49.75 percent) as the primary purpose of sharing, posting, and commenting.

Students' ability to take action upon receiving and evaluating the information on social media was indicated in the survey by the question asking them to mark actions they have taken invoked by certain information. The figure above shows limited civil participation, where only 10.5 percent of the respondents reported "participation in protests and demonstrations," 21 percent reported "participating in meetings and gathering," and 15.3 percent reported "petitioning and signing, while sharing with others," whereas discussing with friends and family (47.85 percent) and donating (50.7 percent) were marked by a larger number of the respondents, as shown in the figure above.

Positive acts, such as donating, sharing, and discussing were self-reported more frequently by the respondents than critical or radical acts, such as protesting, demonstrating, and petitioning. Media researchers reported that social media tend to be common "virtue signaling" spaces. The "friendship-driven" nature of young people's engagement or the desirability of belonging when they engage on social media has been reported by media researchers in the US, for example (Clark and Marchi 2017). Young people's apparent limited acts upon civic engagement are also influenced by the uncertainty of the algorithms of the platforms, as well as the regulations and surveillance of social media by authorities.

Media scholars acknowledge that young people's engagement with digital technology has transformative potential for increasing agency and creating collective meaning (Kafai and Peppler 2010; Reitsamer and Zobl 2014). At the same time, cognitive scientists are increasingly warning how young people's increased agility in visual literacy, spatial orientation, and multitasking due to visual media and video games might be coming at the expense of diminished ability in sustained deep reflection and inductive analysis (Carr 2010; Greenfield 2009; Turkle 2008, 2012). Reflective and critical abilities to contribute to civic discourse and to discern the hidden agendas behind commercial and ideological speech online are paramount media literacy skills for young people.

Young people use the platforms for their artistic and creative expression, but they are aware that the algorithms and regulations of the platforms are beyond their control. The students interviewed are aware of the enabling but, at the same time, rapidly changing affordances of social media. An aspiring social media entrepreneur and master student, Bagi, who has a big following on TikTok and YouTube teaching social media use, compares the two platforms and the challenges of using them by saying:

> TikTok's algorithm is easier and designed so that it keeps people scrolling. YouTube changes its algorithm often, and it is hard to break into YouTube … That is why we reduced our YouTube content almost ten times. YouTube's content regulation is stricter, and it abides by other countries' laws like "only for kids" content with limited ads and product placement … YouTube's policy in place since 2020 requires a length of almost eight minutes to place an ad and tax is being added on YouTube for artists. That is why the tractions on YouTube for us has gotten smaller, and CPM [cost per million] is less, and it has become difficult for artists like us. (interviewee with Bagi, May 24 2022)

Bagi elaborates upon an uneasy truce of using social media to conduct business in Mongolia while social media's algorithmic and economic regulations change. He also expressed that he would like to make sure that the artists use social media to their advantage, and not have social media platforms use them. The conundrum of whether we are using social media or are the raw material of big social media, as Zuboff (2019) elaborated in her surveillance capitalism book, is evident.

Social media platforms accumulate and mine personal data and interactions by utilizing machine learning and data-driven algorithms. This situation creates epistemological asymmetry, where social media corporations know everything about the users, but users know little about them (Baym 2015; Reviglio and Agosti 2020; Zuboff 2019). Users are constantly nudged and tuned into viewing polarizing content and sensational news. Even though social media platforms have increased viral communication and deliberative possibilities, in recent years media scholars throughout the world have documented how social media use a) contributes to "the disinformation order" by spreading false information virally (Bennett and Livingston 2018; Internet Society 2017), b) amplifies the "echo chambers" of extremist political views (Matuszewski and Szabó 2019; Tufekci 2018), and c) undermines democratic discourse by targeting voters with propaganda (Pickard 2017; Woolley and Howard 2016). In the section below, I explore the awareness and practices of young Mongolians in evaluating misinformation, disinformation, and privacy impingement, and their fact-checking practices and media literacy levels.

Digital Pitfalls, Misinformation, and Disinformation

During the elections in Mongolia, campaigns and political attacks fill the public sphere on social media. Since the 2012 election, political campaigns employed and mobilized students and young people to create several media accounts and disseminated tailored messages to specific Facebook group members, and these practices peaked during the 2016 parliamentary election and the 2017 presidential elections. A student, who wants to remain anonymous and served in the military before coming to a university, talks about his experience of working for a political campaign:

> When I worked for an election campaign, I did not use my real account. Instead, I created five different accounts to write comments on election-related posts. I saw that we do not have young and strong candidates in politics and how money pushes people to the top. It is not about the truth or justice ... the whole country consumes fake or superficial things, and ... I even got paid handsomely for using my fake accounts. (Student interview April 6, 2022).

Unknown to the interviewee at that time, these practices of targeting voters to promote candidates and attack political rivals was documented by political communication scholars and called "the disinformation order" (Bennett and Livingston 2018; Pickard 2017). The 2016 and 2017 elections saw public relations companies claiming to have "500k accounts with that many followers and 100k Likes or other engagement metrics" (Baasanjav 2020). One of the journalists I interviewed said that journalists had information concerning a group of people creating false accounts on Facebook and attacking others on behalf of politicians as a part of campaigns. But, the burden of proof is on journalists, whilst the elites in power sue them for slander and defamation. These election practices appear to be from the "informational operation playbook," which has been on the rise globally.[5]

Bennett and Livingston (2018) define disinformation as "intentional falsehoods spread as news stories or simulated documentary formats to advance political goals" (124). Online election interference and "informational operations' involving state actors, enterprising news businesses, troll factories, hacker groups and bots have been on the rise globally ("Rise of Digital Authoritarianism" 2018; ITU 2018; Damarad and Yeliseyeu 2018). Politicians and their campaigns benefited from social media utilizing bots and automated posts, but smear attacks from their opponents also targeted them. In a postcommunist society recuperating from ubiquitous propaganda and extensive surveillance, speaking out and standing for beliefs is dangerous. At the same time, astroturfing manufactured in favor of the elites spreads. In other words, the social construction of digital civic discourse in Mongolia takes the "path-dependency" of socialist-era fears of surveillance and is restricted by existing routines of institutions. Political discourse is flooded and distracted by slander and undocumented squabbles. Vaccari and Chadwick (2020), who analyzed improved deepfakes and "inadvertent dissemination misinformation" on social media, claim that these uncertainties contribute mainly to the low levels of trust in news and general cynicism among the public. This conclusion is highly relevant to the analysis of digital space discourse in Mongolia.

The young people in Mongolia are sensitive and often recognize the pitfalls of digital media in political situations, and they believe that social media, especially Facebook, has many trolls during the election periods. In general, as of 2022, college students are aware of the prevalence of misinformation, as shown by their self-reported responses to the question, "How often do you encounter mis/disinformation on social media?" According to their responses, 76.2 percent or 177 respondents (out of $N = 239$) said that they either "Frequently" (56.1 percent) or "Always" (20.9 percent of respondents)

5 See Damarad and Yeliseyeu (2018); "Rise of Digital Authoritarianism" (2018); and ITU (2018) on the rise of election-related informational operations globally.

encounter dis/misinformation.[6] They are often confident that they know how to identify dis/misinformation indicated by their answers to the question "How do you check dis/misinformation?" Eighty-six respondents or 38.9 percent ($N = 221$) reported that they know the ways to fact-check and the most common way of fact-checking (77.38 percent of the respondents) was checking with media sources. Only sixteen students, or 7.2 percent of respondents, selected the "I don't know" option.

The youth self-reported a higher level of confidence in recognizing misinformation, but when asked using an open-ended question to write their practices of checking, the majority of respondents wrote that they check with journalistic sources (around one-half of those who answered this open-ended question), sixty-eight students said that they check whether the media reported it, and forty-eight answered that they check whether the source on social media is an official address. Only a few wrote that they would compare multiple sources or check pictures, facts, and videos. Of the respondents, 24 percent said they either did not know how to check or did not respond to the question. These answers show that, despite the confidence they self-report in recognizing misinformation, they still need media literacy education and guidance. This fact itself points toward the need for general media literacy education.

Despite young people's always-on access to digital media, they are seldom reflective of their media experiences. Young people often share and distribute information without carefully filtering and evaluating it. One of the interviewees, a senior studying media, expresses how his peers are quick to share information they find on social media by saying:

> My peers immediately, in 2–3 seconds, share sensational and false information on Messenger chats, TikTok, and Snapchat without checking the facts ... Before the war in Ukraine, my friend sent me messages worried about the war even before it started. The video he sent me had video-game footage instead of an on-ground report. False and misleading information is "puffed" and widespread on social media. (interview with Tugi, March 11 2022)

As students develop their media literacy skills in college, they assess information more critically, and their agency to take responsibility and meaningfully participate grows. The interviewees acknowledged that all

6 Their responses are recorded on the scale of 1 to 5, 1 being "Never" to 5 being "Always" (Baasanjav et.al. 2022).

media use increased during the COVID-19 pandemic, partially due to the confinement of COVID-19 restraints when whole families stayed at home. Furthermore, during the COVID pandemic, the government tightened regulations on online websites and social media platforms, criminalized the distribution of "obviously false information," and allowed only "official source" information during the evening news. These measures contributed to the decreased trust in social, as well as in traditional media.

Even though young people's use and understanding of social media vary widely in general, they mostly consume information on their smartphones using social media rather than through traditional media like television or newspapers. The interviewees said they read newspapers only when required to do so in class. As for television, they say they "stopped watching television" because they "do not have the time to spend waiting to watch a specific program." But during the COVID pandemic, when students stayed at home, they watched television.

However, when the students were asked about their trust in information on both social and traditional media on a scale of one to ten, one being "not trusting at all" to ten being "deeply trusting," a significantly higher level of trust in the information on traditional media was reported with the mean score of $M = 6.5$ ($SD = 1.7$) than students' level of trust in information on social media with the mean score of $M = 4.79$ ($SD = 1.59$). The difference is analyzed using the t-test, where a significant difference between the mean scores ($M = 6.5$ for traditional media and $M = 4.79$ for social media) was tested for significance in SPSS ($t(236) = 46.4, p < 0.001$, Cohens' $d = 1.59$) (Baasanjav et al. 2022). The interviewees also confirmed by stating that traditional media, especially television, has more trustworthiness than social media.

Another surprising contestation area emerged in the survey regarding youth perception of privacy and safety of personal information on social media. Contrary to the assumption that young people are less concerned about private information disclosure, the survey results show differently. Of the respondents, 64.2 percent are not at ease with giving fingerprints and citizen registration numbers online, while the other 15 percent think that the government and companies are collecting too much information. Yet, 24.45 percent feel unable to resist because they cannot do much about informational privacy. It was legal until 2022 for banks and mobile operators to use fingerprints and citizen registration numbers. In other words, these data show that young people are concerned about their privacy and personal information but feel powerless. This concern was also commented on by one of the interviewees:

> Our office lost its Facebook page account password. Someone from China logged in and changed the account to "WallMart online." So, we set up two-factor authentication and changed the password. Now, I see another department at school lost its password. Someone has been posting gaming posts on the page for a month now ... People are joking and do not take security risks seriously. (interviewee with Mugi, May 24, 2022)

The interviewee is apprehensive about her work account safety and the two-factor authentication system that should be taken more seriously, but she also realizes the technological challenges of fixing the issue. Media literacy education on the part of citizens and clear laws and regulations are essential for reducing uncertainty on social media platforms.

In recent years, Facebook has been investigated in the US for its invasive tracking of users, its role in far-right group congregation, and its enabling of the spread of misinformation and disinformation on its platform. Despite the investigations, Facebook's profits soared, reaching nearly eighty-six-billion dollars in 2020, and the corporation's usual business operates by packaging its 2.6 billion users worldwide to advertisers (Ovide 2021).

Psuedopolls and Technological Populism

Political elites appeal to the young population, who increasingly participate in online and social media, by conducting media polls to legitimize their actions and create an image of more technologically progressive and democratic governance. Mongolia's elites are adapting to the "hybridized" media system by embracing some media pluralism and seeking some veneer of legitimacy, as media scholars observed in other countries (See Schedler 2013; Chadwick 2017; Voltmer et al. 2021). Following these scholars' arguments on the changes in how political information is produced and circulated, below I bring up a couple of examples of legitimacy-seeking pseudopolls and the rise of populism online in Mongolia.

In 2022, I was on a field trip in Ulaanbaatar when the city was forging into normal life from the long-time COVID-19 restraints. The traffic congestion, one of Ulaanbaatar's major problems for a while now, was exacerbated by in-class sessions of elementary and secondary schools. A public announcement about an online poll aired during the evening news program on the national broadcaster's prime time news show *MNB News*. City Mayor Dolgorsürengiin Sumiyabazar asked frustrated parents and the public to vote to either "Support" or "Don't Support" the decision to change the starting and ending hours of some schools (Bolor 2022). The public announcement was also advertised on other leading websites like Mongolian news wire services at montsame.mn. Thirty-six out of fifty-nine schools mentioned in the news are private schools in relatively better-off districts of Ulaanbaatar and 29 percent of parents of the kids in these schools drive or use cabs, according to the article on the website of the government news wire services. The poll gave voice to the relatively upper echelon of the city whose children attend private schools and who drive their children to school, but it did not result in any noticeable actions. Technically, the one-click poll with only two options to support or to not support the decision enables one person, for example, to vote multiple times from different devices or other browsers on the same device, leaving the reliability and validity of the poll questionable. Pseudopolls remain a popular act among political elites as they give purported legitimacy to their actions.

Sumiyabazar's poll has a precedent. In 2015, then prime minister and former television show host, Chimediin Saikhanbileg, conducted a four-day text message referendum on the OT mining contract, asking for the public's input to either proceed with the contract or reject it. A text message poll to solve the impasse of OT, the biggest foreign investment contract the Mongolian government signed, received considerable attention in international media. Chimediin Saikhanbileg, who became a parliamentarian and the prime minister (2014–6), campaigned on his experience as the chairman of the CITA from 2004–8. He also led several e-government initiatives and foresaw telecommunications company contracts with transnational companies during his leadership in the organization. Considering his background, the act was a stunt to please investors in Rio Tinto, a big Canadian-based mining corporation, and Ivanhoe Mines of the United States.

This mobile phone referendum was criticized for the low participation of the public, yet international media saw, in this case, a noteworthy attempt to expand public discourse using mobile technology to rural populations who were traditionally excluded but now had the means to participate (Edwards 2015; Hahn 2018). Only 10 percent of the population participated in the poll because it was not clear how the results of the poll would be used in any decision. The inappropriateness of the wording in the question was another factor that turned people away. The question in the poll only allowed the participants two options: 1) to increase a debt ceiling or 2) go through an economic austerity. Hahn (2018) compares the text referendum to the historical plebiscite of 1945 by which the Chinese Kuomintang government under Chiang Kai-shek accepted Mongolia's independence. She argues that the text message poll was a worthy attempt to solve an impossible situation by asking the public, considering the high literacy rate of the population, widespread use of mobile phones (120 percent of the population has mobile phones), and the relatively open political culture. The 1945 plebiscite is recognized in history textbooks as a national referendum that was crucial to the country's independence. It was clearly a divergent media pattern from the Soviet-modeled media's soliciting input from the public. Saikhanbileg's government signed a contract with Rio Tinto, later known as the infamous Dubai contract. Since then, several Mongolian governments have renegotiated with the multinational mines to alleviate the contract's damages and have even gone through international arbitration courts, as I discussed in chapter 3.

The roles of online polls in the outcomes of the mining impasse are not clear. Neither are their roles in broader policy discourse in general. Because politicians often resort to similar "quick tech fixes," these polls should be critically examined in social and cultural contexts. In the previous chapter, I showed how populism is an inherent discourse of democracy and how both elites and "the masses" have dominating and "resisting" discourses through populism. Even though online polls resemble online participation, they are also used to collect information from users and provide a façade for politicians. As Voltmer et al. explain (2021), even in an autocracy elites tolerate some media plurality because citizens can pressure them on social media. In 2011, I wrote about how the Mongolian government and civil society organizations chose certain communication patterns among available options by applying Bordewijk and Van Kaam's (2002) four types of media typologies and Van Dijk's (2000) application of different models of democracy (Baasanjav 2011). Before 2010, I found that government organizations and CSOs diverged considerably in their information-producing and circulating patterns; the former mostly broadcasted from the center to the public and facilitated online conversation and dialogue only to a limited extent. In contrast, CSOs used chats and discussion forums significantly more than government organizations. In recent years, we have seen pseudopolls by politicians who tend to appeal to the public and collect information from citizens to legitimize their actions. Van Dijk (2000) called this pattern "infocracy," a governance pattern based on an increasing collection of user information by a state surveillance system. In Mongolia, since this kind of technological surveillance is relatively new, especially over foreign platforms like Facebook, surveillance to exert political pressure is also new and is probably limited. However, if one asks, "Who benefits and what context contributed to the outcomes?" then the semblance of participatory decision-making benefits politicians more than citizens who participated in them without clear outcomes. As surveillance capitalism advances, these patterns can be effectively used by entrenched commercial and political interests in various types of government organizations.

Conclusion

Dramatic economic and political changes are shaping media development and informational spheres in Mongolia; in return, politics and practices are shaped by the media and online civic discourse. This chapter contributes to the understanding of the complex state of digitally mediated discourse in modern Mongolia through interviewees' accounts and survey results among young people. New forms of media technology appeal to Mongolia's young population because they offer new forms of public participation that were not previously available. Young people who have grown up in plural media environments are eager to express and participate, but the uncertainties of their actions and digital pitfalls constrain their participation and agency.

In these increasingly complex informational ecosystems, civil society organizations and youth in Mongolia navigate social media variedly. I discussed how investigative journalists, women, and environmental NGOs took advantage of social media affordances, yet their practices were constrained by structural deficiencies of resources and social stratification that are increasing rapidly. An increasing number of profit-seeking and enterprising organizations on social media, particularly on Facebook, mislead civic discourse and hurt young people with misinformation.

When faced with the unprecedented challenges of social media in political discourse, some politicians have the impulse to curb and control social media, partially following Chinese and Russian regulatory frameworks. Other politicians cater to the opinion polls in order to garner support or, most likely, to legitimize their actions. The infocracy tendency (Bordewijk and Van Kaam 2002; Van Dijk 2000) provides apparent legitimacy without clear outcomes on how these polls and opinions factor into the decision-making of politicians. This veneer of online participation without analysis and policy outcomes does not increase public discussion but allows citizens to vent. The internet arrived in Mongolia well after its commercialization in the late 1990s, and, in general, it lacked civil society groups and academic community participation like The WELL and USENET, which played major roles in fostering civic discourse on the internet in its earlier stages in the West. The takeover of social media over the public discourse in the form of pseudopolls discussed in this chapter provides some appearance of participatory culture.

However, only a small percentage of citizens participate in these polls, and the policy ramifications of these polls are never revealed because they do not lead to policy outcomes.

Work Cited

ADB. 2019. "Civil Society Brief: Mongolia." https://www.adb.org/sites/default/files/publication/503101/civil-society-brief-mongolia.pdf.

Agre, Philip E. 2002. "Real-Time Politics: The Internet and the Political Process." *The Information Society* 18 (5): 311–31.

Arceneaux, Phillip C. and Lucian F. Dinu. 2018. "The Social Mediated Age of Information: Twitter and Instagram as Tools for Information Dissemination in Higher Education." *New Media & Society* 20 (11): 4155–76.

Baasanjav, Undrah. 2008. "Mediated Political and Social Participation: Examining the Use of the Internet by Mongolian Government and Civil Society Institutions." *The Journal of Information Technology and Politics* 4 (3): 41–60.

———. 2011. "Web Use Patterns for Civic Discourse: The Case of Mongolian Institutions." *Information, Communication and Society* 14 (5): 591–618.

Baasanjav, Undrah, Dashdondog Iderjargal, Tugj Unursaikhan, Norovsuren Ariunzaya, Boldbaatar Bayarmaa, and Ganbaatar Mendkhuu. 2022. "Digital Repertoire of Young Mongolian People and Transcultural Implications." Paper presented to the IAMCR pre-conference "Digital Governance and Transcultural Communications." July 2022. https://xwcb.bnu.edu.cn/sn/ln/132189.html.

Baasanjav, Undrah, Poul Nielsen, and Munkhmandakh Myagmar. 2024. "Patronage Media in Post-Communist Mongolia." *Central European Journal of Communication* 17 (2(36)): 247–67.

Baym, Nancy. K. 2015. "Social Media and The Struggle for Society." *Social Media + Society* 1 (1). https://doi.org/doi:10.1177/2056305115580477.

Beck, Linda, Toby Mendel, and Jeff Thindwa. 2007. *The Enabling Environment for Social Accountability in Mongolia.* The International Bank for Reconstruction and Development. https://forum.mn/uploads/site/1126/res_mat/SocialAccountability.pdf.

Bennett, W. Lance and Steven Livingston. 2018. "The Disinformation Order: Disruptive Communication and the Decline of Democratic Institutions." *European Journal of Communication* 33 (2): 122–39.

Bolor, J. 2022. 59 сургуулийн хичээл эхлэх цагийг өөрчлөх асуудлаар санал авч эхэллээ [A poll opened to change school hours of 59 schools]. Monstsame, Feb 16. https://www.montsame.mn/mn/read/289856.

Bordewijk, Jan L. and Ben V. Kaam. 2002. "Toward a New Classification of Tele-Information Services." In *McQuail's Reader in Mass Communication Theory*, edited by Denis McQuail, 113–25. SAGE.

Boyd, Danah. 2010. "Social Network Sites as Networked Publics: Affordances, Dynamics, and Implications." In *A Networked Self: Identity, Community, and Culture on Social Network Sites*, edited by Zizi Papacharissi. 39–58. Routledge.

Bucher, Taina and Anne Helmond. 2017. "The Affordances of Social Media Platforms." In *The SAGE Handbook of Social Media*, edited by Jean Burgess, Alice Marwick and Thomas Poell, 233–53. SAGE.

Carr, Nicholas. 2010. *The Shallows: What the Internet Is Doing to Our Brains*. W. W. Norton.

Chadwick, Andrew. 2017. *The Hybrid Media System: Politics and Power.* 2nd ed. Oxford University Press. https://doi.org/10.1093/oso/9780190696726.001.0001.

Clark, Lynn S. and Regina Marchi. 2017. *Young People and the Future of News.* Cambridge University Press.

Damarad, Volha and Andrei Yeliseyeu. 2018. *Disinformation Resilience in Central and Eastern Europe.* Eurasian States in Transition research center. prismua.org/wp-content/uploads/2018/06/DRI_CEE_2018.pdf.

Davaasharav, Munkhchimeg and Peter Bittner. 2018. "Mongolians protest to demand greater action against child abuse." Reuters, March 31. https://www.reuters.com/article/world/mongolians-protest-to-demand-greater-action-against-child-abuse-idUSKBN1H7098/

Edwards, Terrence. 2015. "Mongolian 'Text Referendum' Backs Mine Investment Over Austerity." Reuters, Feb. 3. https://www.reuters.com/article/us-mongolia-investment-vote/mongolian-text-referendum-backs-mine-investment-over-austerity-idUSKBN0L809A20150204.

Galis, Vasilis and Christina Neumayer. 2016. "Laying Claim to Social Media by Activists: A Cyber-Material *Détournement*." *Social Media + Society* 2 (3). https://doi.org/10.1177/2056305116664360.

Gitlin, Todd. 1980. *The Whole World Is Watching.* University of California Press.

GlobalStats. 2019. Social Media Stats Mongolia. Accessed May 2020 http://gs.statcounter.com/social-media-stats/all/mongolia.

Greenfield, Patricia M. 2009. "Technology and Informal Education: What is Taught, What is Learned." *Science* 323 (5910): 69–71.

Hahn, Alisson. 2018. "Mongolia's 2015 Referendum via Text Messaging: Engaging Rural and Nomadic Citizens in Public Screen Deliberation." *International Journal of Communication* 12 (2018): 4379–4400.

Internet Society. 2017. *Global Internet Report 2017: Path to Our Digital Future.* https://www.internetsociety.org/resources/doc/2017/global-internet-report-2017/

ITU. 2018. *Global Cybersecurity Index 2018.* https://www.itu.int/dms_pub/itu-d/opb/str/D-STR-GCI.01-2018-PDF-E.pdf

Kafai, Yasmin and Kylie Peppler. 2011. "Youth, Technology, and DIY: Developing Participatory Competencies in Creative Media Production." *Review of Research in Education* 35: 89–119. https://doi.org/10.3102/0091732X10383211.

Kaldor, Mary. 2008. "Democracy and Globalization." In *Global Civil Society 2007/8*, edited by Martin Albrow, Helmut Anheier, Marlies Glasius, Monroe Price and Mary Kaldor, 34-45. SAGE.

Keane, John. 2003. *Global Civil Society?* Cambridge University Press.

Lokot, Tetyana. 2020. "Articulating Networked Citizenship on the Russian Internet: A Case for Competing Affordances." *Social Media + Society* 6 (4): 1–12. https://doi.org/10.1177/2056305120984459.

Matuszewski, Paweł and Gabriella Szabó. 2019. "Are Echo Chambers Based on Partisanship? Twitter and Political Polarity in Poland and Hungary." *Social Media + Society* 5 (2): 1–14. https://doi.org/10.1177/2056305119837671.

Misheel, B. 2019. "Facebook to Cooperate with CRC to Fight Fake News." Montsame, April 2. https://montsame.mn/en/read/184925.

Norris, Pippa. 2001. *Digital Divide: Civic Engagement, Information Poverty, and the Internet Worldwide.* Cambridge UP.

Ofcom. 2021. *Adult's Media Use and Attitude Report.* https://www.ofcom.org.uk/siteassets/resources/documents/research-and-data/media-literacy-research/adults/adults-media-use-and-attitudes-2021/adults-media-use-and-attitudes-report-2020-21.pdf?v=326334.

Ovide, Shira. 2021. "Facebook Is Hated — and Rich." *New York Times*, Jan 26. https://www.nytimes.com/2021/01/28/technology/facebook-earnings-reputation.html.

Pickard, Victor. 2017. "The Big Picture: Misinformation Society." *Public Books*, Nov. 28. http://www.publicbooks.org/the-big-picture-misinformation-society/.

Pickard, Victor. 2022. "Can Journalism Survive in the Age of Platform Monopolies? Confronting Facebook's Negative Externalities." In *Digital Platform Regulation: Global Perspectives on Internet Governance*, edited by Terry Flew and Fiona Martin, 23–41. Palgrave Global Media Policy and Business. Palgrave Macmillan. https://doi.org/10.1007/978-3-030-95220-4_2.

PIM. 2022. *Mongolian Media Today.* Ulaanbaatar: PIM.

Poell, Thomas and José van Dijck. 2015. "Social Media and Activist Communication." In *The Routledge Companion to Alternative and Community Media*, edited by Chris Atton, 527–37. Routledge.

Reitsamer, Rosa and Elke Zobl. 2014. "Alternative Media Production, Feminism, and Citizenship Practices." In *DIY Citizenship: Critical Making and Social Media*, edited by Matt Ratto and Megan Boler, 329–42. MIT Press.

Reviglio, Urbano and Claudio Agosti. 2020. "Thinking Outside the Black-Box: The Case For 'Algorithmic Sovereignty' in Social Media." *Social Media + Society* 6 (2). https://doi.org/10.1177/2056305120915613.

Rheingold, Howard. 2000. *The Virtual Community: Homesteading on the Electronic Frontier.* MIT Press.

Richez, Emmanuelle, Vincent Raynauld, Abunya Agi, and Arief B. Kartolo. 2020. "Unpacking the Political Effects of Social Movements with a Strong Digital Component: The case of #IdleNoMore in Canada." *Social Media + Society* 6 (2). https://doi.org/10.1177/2056305120915588.

"The Rise of Digital Authoritarianism: Fake News, Data Collection, and the Challenge to Democracy." Freedom House, October 31, 2018. https://freedomhouse.org/article/rise-digital-authoritarianism-fake-news-data-collection-and-challenge-democracy.

Schedler, Andreas. 2013. *The Politics of Uncertainty: Sustaining and Subverting Electoral Authoritarianism.* Oxford University Press.

Tufekci, Zeynep. 2018. "YouTube, The Great Radicalizer." *New York Times*, March 10. https://www.nytimes.com/2018/03/10/opinion/sunday/youtube-politics-radical.html.

Turkle, Sherry. 2008. "Always-On/Always-On-You: Tethered Self." In *Handbook of Mobile Communication Studies*, edited by James Katz, 121–37. MIT Press.

Turkle, Sherry. 2012. *Alone Together: Why We Expect More from Technology and Less From Each Other.* Basic Books.

Vaccari, Christian and Andrew Chadwick. 2020. "Deepfakes and Disinformation: Exploring the Impact of Synthetic Political Video on Deception, Uncertainty, and Trust in News." *Social Media + Society* 6 (1). https://doi.org/10.1177/2056305120903408.

Van Dijk, Jan. 2000. "Models of Democracy and Concepts of Communication." In *Digital Democracy: Issues of Theory and Practice*, edited by Kenneth L. Hacker and Jan van Dijk, 30-53. SAGE.

Voltmer, Katrin, Kjetil Selvik, and Jacob Høigilt. 2021. "Hybrid Media and Hybrid Politics: Contesting Informational Uncertainty in Lebanon and Tunisia." *The International Journal of Press/Politics* 26 (4): 842–60. https://doi.org/10.1177/1940161221999266.

Woolley, Sam and Philip Howard. 2016. "Political Communication, Computational Propaganda, and Autonomous Agents." *International Journal of Communication* 10 (2016): 4882–90.

Zuboff, Shoshana. 2019. *The Age of Surveillance Capitalism: The Fight for a Human Future at the New Frontier of Power.* Public Affairs.

Conclusion

This book is an effort to make sense of the rapid media development and changes in the informational sphere in the context of the last thirty years following the democratic revolution. Throughout the book, I argued that media and technological acceleration, along with political and economic changes, shape modern Mongolian culture. Today, Mongolians flock together in the virtual app ClubHouse to support candidates during the elections, and herdsmen/women in the countryside sell cashmere after they check the prices on their cell phones or Twitter (now X). The political and economic participation of Mongolians in civic discourse has dramatically shifted from the socialist-era practices of attending "morning newspaper reading hours" (*өглөөний сонсгол*) of the party newspapers and listening to polished radio programs about the workers "building socialism" over the cable radios. Instead, as in other countries, Mongolian users are resourceful and savvy; they have eagerly "saddled" onto social media as they did their horses to take advantage of mobility, speed, and spatiality. Informational platforms, Facebook, Instagram, X (formerly Twitter), and TikTok are in the hands of most Mongolians, who generally enjoy civil liberty, online cultural expressions, and private property rights guaranteed in the constitution of 1992.

At an unprecedented pace, the hybrid media environment mirrors and shapes political communication, economic outlook, institutional norms, and Mongolian identity. The Mongolian elite also imagine replicating the "Asian tiger" phenomenon utilizing the informational economy. The Asian economic development news, along with the cultural programs from the distant West as well as from China, Japan, and Korea that were not available during the socialist era, now fill the airtime of television and cable networks and the social media feeds of young people. As Mongolian audiences who grew up in the converged media environment immerse themselves in global and regional media, they distance themselves from the Soviet past. These developments co-occur with new challenges such as the lowered trust in institutions and the co-optation of media by the authorities in Mongolia, similar to development in other countries. I conclude the book

Undrah Baasanjav, *Information Society and Media Development in Modern Mongolia*.
Taylor & Francis Group, 2025
DOI: 10.5117/9789463729888_CONC

by summarizing the role of globalization on the Mongolian informational sphere and identity, the geopolitical influences of its neighbors, and some new challenges concerning the spread of global informational capitalism. As this book is couched in the framework of media studies and the political economy of an information society, I also point toward critical issues of these developments including the increased state intervention into media spheres and the rise of the commercialization and surveillance by state and corporate global actors. The changing civic sphere in recent years in Mongolia is characterized by new types of technopopulism along with techno-utopian views of the younger generation. Elites seek legitimacy by tolerating some dissident communication and appealing to populism using tools such as pseudopolls in the public discourse. In this fluid and negotiated sphere, many young Mongolians need more guidance in developing critical literacy skills.

Globalization, Hybrid Media Spheres, and Mongolian Identity

Throughout the book, I argued that the Mongolian informational sphere has been influenced by globalization, international governance institutions, and global media companies via their policies and media content. Since the opening of the market, Western and foreign news and cultural products such as CNN, MTV, and Netflix have been part of the media diets of new generations. Media content produced abroad, particularly in Korea, has started to influence Mongolian identity, pulling them away from the Soviet past.

Korean entertainment aesthetics, extended family values, and the consumer lifestyle appeal to Mongolians, many of whom also have family members and relatives working in Korea. As of 2019, as many as 50.8-thousand Mongolians out of 197 thousand living outside of the country worked and studied in South Korea, according to the Ministry of Foreign Affairs. The remittance money from Mongolians working outside of the country is up to 3.7 percent of the GDP, a significant amount of this coming from the South Korean diaspora.[1] At least eight to ten universities in Mongolia teach the Korean language, and Mongolians in Korea assimilate the culture relatively quickly and "pass" for "residents" because of the ethnic similarity and cultural proximity. Almost half of the Mongolians in Korea study in

1 Dolgormaa & Kisun (2023) https://www.degruyter.com/document/doi/10.1515/modi-2021-010104/html

colleges and universities, and Mongolians in South Korea bring in new technology and cultural capital because South Korea has become the leading country in internet broadband development and mobile phone use. Furthermore, like Koreans, Mongolians started to enjoy ownership of their apartments, cars, and consumer goods. Korea was an inspiring Asian tiger nation with a Western-like lifestyle, which splintered successfully from the North Korean communist past.

It is not surprising that the Mongolian media market is fertile soil for cultural products coming from complex media environments like Korea. Mongolia has structural constraints such as a small audience and the lack of credit-financing systems that strap the financial independence and viability of media organizations. In an established media market, television programs are often deficit financed, borrowing money upfront and making up the expenses and profits from advertisements, and resale and leasing, also known as syndication, to different stations, cable channels, and streaming services. This way, the financial dependence on single sponsors and political patronages of television stations is balanced by multiple sponsors and advertisers who guarantee the financial independence of the station. In this broadcast model, viewership, market competition, and program rating all factor into renewing broadcast licenses. That is why the regulator is supposed to select the national broadcasters that can produce quality programs that sustain and even create profits using these financial tools. This model works when the legal environment protects the copyrights of the authors and creators, financial credits are available for producers to create programs, and a syndication market exists for selling and leasing the programs for redistribution. However, in Mongolia copyright law is weak, the credit system is rudimentary, and the syndication market for creative programs does not exist. The media market in Mongolia is a mixed bag of unregulated commercial potentials, politically affiliated media, untrained professionals, and rudimentary payments involving cash and even barter trades, as I discussed in chapter 2. That is why, even though there is an increase in the number of media outlets, especially online outlets, only a few of them have content-creating capabilities, while many recycle the content and news of established news organizations and television content. MNB and other socialist-era media institutions still have residual market power, to which the political elites cling with their government and political support.

The tensions between old and new, as well as national and international, can be seen in broadcasting, which used to be strictly controlled by the state. MNB's *Evening News Hours* is still the leading national news, and

Naadam festivities' broadcasting of the traditional Mongolian men's three games (*Eriin Gurvan Naadam*) of wrestling, horse racing, and archery is the most popular television program (Maxima Consulting 2020). In these traditional programs, one can see the persistence of the path dependency from the socialist-era media in that the news crews of MNB follow the politicians when they visit their constituencies in the countryside, and these trips are considered "news" even during the election years. The socialist-era institutional routines among journalists continue to reside in their self-censoring practices and politicians' patronizing of media. Traditional, patriarchal, and nationalistic presentations targeting males marginalize women and sexual and ethnic minorities. Along with these traditional programs, international networks from Bloomberg Financial News or Eagle TV to Mongolian new media organizations such as Mongol TV and TenGer TV (formerly Ekh Oron) provide business and international and domestic news analyses. Program franchises including Mongol TV's *Voice of Mongolia*, an adaptation of the international talent show started as *Mongolia's Got Talent* (Mongol TV, 2015–), and Education TV's improvisational comedy *Thank God You Are Here*, in which a celebrity improvises a performance in a surprise situational comedy scene, have counterweighted Korean and Chinese drama series that flooded the market.

The above examples of the media show that Mongolians have broken away from the socialist pattern of no ownership, limited consumption, and frugal spending. Even new Mongols, who own private cottages, luxury cars, private mines, and have foreign-school-educated children, have emerged in the last thirty years of the market economy like "new Russians" or the "black collar class" in China. However, despite the transition to a market economy intensified by commercialized media, consumer education in credit systems, budgets, and media literacy education are very rudimentary or nonexistent in the educational system of the country. In the thirty years of the market economy, the educational system has changed slowly, providing limited consumer education and critical media literacy explaining the differences between commercial and editorial content, partisan press, or ideological influences of media. Books and magazines in the Mongolian language, as well as access to libraries, were historically very limited; thus, the critical examination of texts and humanities education was generally less valued during the seventy years of socialism. When international news became available to Mongolians, from British BBC to German DW to American CNN, the audience lacked the English language ability. Local media translated news and stories for the audience selectively, leaving out most of the critical analysis or providing it to a very limited extent. Most people focused on providing day-to-day food staples, and school economics classes were taught focusing on carpentry for boys and cooking and sewing for girls.

Mongolian media spheres have increasingly been influenced by inflows of capital, services, and products by giant mining or technology multinationals like Facebook, Google, and Microsoft, as I discussed in chapters 1 and 3. The internet, social media, and other content delivery options like Netflix and Hulu have brought global media companies like Facebook and Google the duopoly in online marketing, taking approximately 67 percent of world advertisement money in 2021. Globalization discontent and identity changes manifest themselves in media texts by invoking xenophobic and nationalistic sentiments in rap lyrics and dramas, as well as in activities by groups like *Dayar Mongol* (pan-mongolism) (Billé 2015; "Racism in Mongolia" 2012). "Globalization-from-below" (Flew 2020) has also occurred, and Mongolian cultural products, movies, music, and books have started to spread to the world market on YouTube, Spotify, and National Geographic, owing mostly to the internet and social media. Exported media texts involving music and videos seldom represent the traditional Mongolian identity of the nomadic heritage, untapped pastureland, and the thirteen-century epic stories of Chinggis Khan. These representations contrast with twenty-first-century Asian identities Mongolians aspire to emulate following the Asian economic prosperity and Korean cultural popularity. Cultural backlashes and xenophobia reached their height during the mining boom when foreign coal and gold mines and their construction work were contracted to foreign companies, as I discussed in chapters 3 and 5. These factors profoundly influence media organizations, their content and funding, and the general media sphere. Media professionals and journalists are aware of the tremendous influences of mining and big media companies, and professional ethics codes and legal protection for investigative journalism and whistleblowing have recently been developed.

In the online media sphere, citizens' engagement has become vital for political communication and dissidence, as I discussed in chapters 4 and 5. Both elites and citizens participate for legitimacy and to be heard. I argue that many digital-born sites and legacy media online news sites operate on a shoestring budget and the financial vulnerability makes them easy to be instrumentalized by politicians. As the commercialization and surveillance on these platforms increases around the world, media literacy skills and critical examination of potential pitfalls are of the utmost importance.

Government Intervention into Media Spheres and The Public Interest

Political communication is changing due to Mongolia's hybrid media spheres. As media convergence accelerates in Mongolia, elites adopt cyberfuture laws focusing on tightened regulations and security and increased government intervention in the media sphere. A batch of cyberfuture laws was adopted by the parliament in 2022 that criminalized the spreading of false information and increased an undue burden on journalists in defamation cases, as I discussed in chapter 4. In chapter 5, I also showed how political elites use digital technologies and social media to create a semblance of participation as a kind of technopopulism.

To protect from the cultural influences of foreign programs, the government adopted the National Program on Mongolian Creative Content from 2015 to 2025 and amended the Law on Culture by mandating a 50 percent increase in the total amount of Mongolian language content by commercial broadcasters (Parliament of Mongolia 2015). The intent behind the program was to counterweight the flooding of foreign programs and to curb the rising audience for foreign programs, especially Korean dramas on Mongolian television. However, the government interventions to balance global media inflow into the media market with local content did little because of the national program's small annual budget of ten billion tugriks (around five million dollars in 2015). The national program could support approximately ten initiatives a year in creating content in television, media arts, and digital environments. The program increased the number of Mongolian language websites, but it did little for television given the capital-intensive nature of television programs. Even though the program had good intentions, upfront government incentives to produce creative content subverted an equal playing field for businesses when creating media content by subsidizing some—especially some politically affiliated—websites. These state funds made the government the biggest advertiser in the small and financially strapped Mongolian market. This way, the entrenched "reciprocity" or financial dependency between the elite and media has deepened since politicians need media in their campaigns. These government interventions erode the media market and funnel state funds to private media illegitimately.

Government-subsidized content and sponsor-commissioned programs have become prevalent in broadcast and online media in recent years. When the People's Party, one of the two offshoots of the former People's Revolutionary Party, consolidated power in all three government branches, state subsidies and the funding of partisan media increased. Government agencies like the National Public Health Center and the Anti-Corruption Agency have been listed among the top ten advertisers (Maxima Consulting 2020). Through these advertisements, politicians funnel government funds to private media they own. In addition, the percentage of government-owned media increased to 11 percent, and many television and online media sites have political affiliations in their ownership and funding (PIM 2022). A clear example of the state ownership that has not been dismantled is the state news agency Montsame (Mongolian Electronic Wire Services).

Government direct control and interference in media have increased through the political appointments of the directors of the CRC and the governing board members and the executives of MNB (the public service broadcaster). Under the auspices of the e-Mongolia program and Vision 2050,[2] government services, from citizen registration to social welfare systems, have increased in digital forms. With this trend, politicians have tightened their grip on the supposedly independent industry regulator, CRC, which, in return, created unequal media ownership regulations among various digital services selectively, as I discussed in chapter 4. Furthermore, politicians exploit the vagueness of the term "public interest" in the laws and weaponize it to further their political and business interests. For example, the "national security and the public interest" clause that was added to the 2021 Law on Public Information Transparency further enables government organizations to classify information for "restriction" more often than its previous version of 2016. Furthermore, politicians and lawmakers frequently hold hostage the MNB's funding and television license fees as a bargaining chip to appoint the board and executive directors of MNB. MNB has guaranteed editorial and organizational independence according to the Law on Public Service Radio and Television, but the ruling party in the government has a strong political grip on the governing body, the selection of senior management, the funding, and even the editorial policies, as I discussed in chapter 4. In 2021–2, the general director was changed three times, and the chairman of the board was changed twice.

The definition of the public interest has still been left open to multiple interpretations, which allows those in the government to interpret it to further their interests, or to increase surveillance rather than to increase civic participation and human rights development. This situation also leads to a paucity of socially responsible media and programs serving the public.

2 https://www.vision2050.gov.mn/eng/vis5.html

Geopolitics and International Influences

Mongolia balances its foreign relations with its two big neighbors diligently, not only because of the geopolitical disadvantages of being sandwiched between Russia and China but also because of its economic dependency on its two neighbors. China is the biggest investor and trading partner with 90 percent of Mongolia's exports going to China, while Russia is the biggest provider of energy and fuel and has been its historical partner for over one-hundred years. In 2022, the Mongolia-China trade surpassed ten-billion dollars (Erdenetuya 2022), while the Mongolia-Russia trade amounted to two-billion dollars ("Россия и Монголия" 2022). Prime Minister Oyun-Erdene and President Khürelsükh both visited China in 2022 and finalized the railway projects connecting TT to three border ports in Gashuun Shukhait, Züünbayan, and Khangi for transporting coal, iron ore, and copper to China.[3] The mining sector defines one-quarter of the Mongolian economy, and the mining-related decisions influence and quickly get inserted into public discourse, as I discussed in chapter 3. Furthermore, the economic and political alliances between Russia and China have moved to a new level, as indicated by a joint statement of Presidents Putin and Xi in February of 2022. One of the major projects between them is the Power of Siberia 2, a gas pipeline from Russia to China through Mongolia expected to start in 2024. This project is a successor to the Power of Siberia 1 pipeline, the Russian Gazprom project connecting northern China to Siberian gas. Russian and Chinese government-led giant economic projects quickly engulf Mongolia's small mining-dependent economy and might lead to a trade expansion with Russia of up to five billion dollars by 2026 according to TASS, the Russian newswire service. Yet, there are many moving parts: China is concerned about Mongolia's possible alliance with Russia or the West and jeopardizing it, and Russia is pressing Mongolia into the payment systems in rubles, without the intermediary of American dollars or Euros ("Россия и Монголия" 2022).

Culturally, Mongolia's informational sphere has been greatly influenced by both giant neighbors. While there is little research on the viewership of the channels and programs of its neighbors, Mongolian audiences' identification with media coming from the two has been changing. The popularity of Russian media and nostalgia for Soviet-era alliances is indicated in the

3 Murun, G., Feb 5, 2022, Ерөнхий сайд нарын уулзалтаар Гашуунсухайтын төмөр замын өргөн нарийн царигийн маргааныг эцэслэн шийдвэрлэлээ, accessed April 3, 2022 from https://ikon.mn/n/2gha

2020 survey Politbarometer conducted by Luvsandendev Sumati, where 68 percent of Mongolians considered Russia the most reliable partner, while only 6.8 percent named China (Rossabi 2021). Russian television channels Russia-1 and -2, news programs, various Soviet and post-Soviet movies, and entertainment channels are broadcast and carried on cable and satellite channels. In addition, social networks like odnoklassniki.ru are popular, especially among people over forty-five and the elites who graduated from Russian secondary schools and colleges. These audiences speak Russian and a big portion of Mongolians cater to nostalgic "good old-time programs" because of the dramatic changes happening in the country. However, as the influences of the Soviet ideology declined so did the media influence and the audience.

Compared to Russian media that triggers nostalgia, Chinese popular television serials such as *Journey to the West* (1998–9) and *Beijing Youth* (2012–) appeal especially to the younger generation's Asian identity. Chinese television CCTV has been available since the boom of cable television in the 1990s but has not been popular due to the audience's language differences. Only a few Mongolians speak Chinese, but the programs in English coming from Hong Kong and Macau, such as movie box office channels and cartoon networks that distribute movies and cartoons in English on Roku TV and Univision cable, have become popular in Mongolia. Inner Mongolian television, with the traditional Mongolian script, appeals to only a niche audience due to the ideological and dialectic differences. During my field trips to Mongolia in 2019 and 2022, I talked to journalists and media professionals and noticed an increase in the training of journalists and professionals in China since 2009. The professionals are not eager to tell their stories of journalistic training even though many have traveled to China, or they explain that they learned technical or media production skills. The quality of Inner Mongolian film and television media production has been steadily improving. The audience for Chinese series has been rising, according to Maxima Consulting, paralleling the rise of Inner Mongolian Film Studios, which in recent years have increased their media production and translation and dubbing of Chinese films into Mongolian (Fan 2022). Chinese social networks such as QQ or Weibo, have not been picked up by Mongolians due to language differences but TikTok has become very popular throughout the world.

I started the book by discussing the role of media in the construction of Mongolian identity and argued that "Mongolness" is geopolitical along with the argument by Kaplonski (2004) describing it as being different from Chinese and Russian identities. Historically, the nation-states have indoctrinated a national identity that is separate from the ethnic Mongol identity, as Bulag (1998) points out. Global information society surely brought the influences of the "third way" from the West or other countries like Korea. In the hybrid media market of recent years, a whole generation of Mongolians grew up consuming content from distant sources over streaming services like Netflix, Hulu, and YouTube, and on social media Instagram and Facebook. Many of these younger Mongolians, like their peers in other countries, speak English, play *Call of Duty*, and consume and create their own user-generated content, like thirty-second or shorter "snackable" videos on TikTok. In other words, geographical and symbolic linguistic boundaries are being blurred for new generations of Mongolians as the outreach of the global information society expands to Mongolia. These generations of media users are dependent on social media and global informational sphere, as these platforms enable them to choose information and entertainment sources seamlessly from local and distant sources. The consumers of these media diets have increasingly blurred boundaries of national and ethnic identities, and they have fluid symbolic cultural markers.

It is plausible to argue that the internationalization debate of the internet and its governance in relation to language uniformity and diversity, which I discussed in chapter 1, reverberates throughout the world, as well as in the Mongolian informational sphere. Linguistic policies and debates on the internet could be seen as a proxy to cultural identity debates on globalization and localization as more users consume and create media indifferent to geographical localities. Because cultural production, meaning making, and societal participation happen through languages, a burgeoning field has emerged extending human rights to people's online activities and linguistic rights online (Taylor 2016). In this book, I argue that the global internet community has succeeded in including a variety of world languages. Online communication and participation are becoming increasingly multilingual as many Arabic, Chinese, Spanish and other language speakers join the internet. The Mongolian media sphere has been one of those spheres that joined thanks to policies and practices of international organizations like WSIS, UNESCO, various engineering task forces on the internet and ICANN, as I argued in chapters 1 and 2.

From the inclusion of Cyrillic Mongolian letters to the digital transition of television networks, various media governance institutions played roles in the shaping of Mongolia's informational sphere. In information societies, one's personal life is increasingly submerged with one's routine online activities, and a new linguistic rights approach to cyberspace that is gaining ground in international law is very relevant to the Mongolian hybrid media sphere. The proponents of this new approach argue that the UDHR entails language rights because the document recognizes the rights to freedom of expression (Article 19), to fair trial (Article 10), and not to be subjected to arbitrary interference with ... privacy, family, home or correspondence (Article 12) (UN General Assembly 1948). The linguistic rights approach has mostly spread in the European Union, resulting in the recognition of twenty-four official languages and the promotion of language rights for minorities, including Catalonian and Welsh (Trenz 2007). However, this online linguistic diversity approach has a long road to go in Asia. The Mongolian state does not provide textbooks in its ethnic minority Kazakh language even today. The Chinese government required elementary and middle school classes to be taught in Mandarin Chinese in Inner Mongolia in 2020 (Shih 2020). This demarcation between national and ethnic identities in the Asian context has yet to be discussed in the public discourse online.

Language is one of the major identity markers that is politicized by states. Nation-states are often established on the languages of the majority groups and evidence of suppressing minority languages and ethnic groups is plentiful throughout human history. Nation-states "actively disadvantage minority language speakers by ignoring and/or stigmatizing their language varieties, as well as confining them to the private realm" (May 2012). The rights of linguistic minorities in international laws are mostly limited to "tolerance-oriented rights" in the private sphere—that is, to publish their own magazines, establish their own private schools, form their own cultural organizations, and not be discriminated against on the basis of their mother tongue (Kymlicka and Patten 2003). The rights to public funding of minority language schools, or to minority language TV/radio, the right to have judicial proceedings in one's language, or the right to receive government documents in one's own language, have been resisted for a long time. Furthering the use of minority languages in the public realm is the goal of promotion-oriented language rights, and has been at the center of most language conflicts around the world (Kymlicka and Patten 2003). I dwelled on this tension between nation-states and supranational organizations like ICANN in relation to language rights on the internet in chapter 1, and this tension still shapes the media spheres around the world.

Global Information Society and Multinational Tech Giants

Rapid informational development in Mongolia, as I described throughout the book, has influenced generations that have similar outlooks on economic development, media consumption, and identity construction with the rest of the world. Information technology and social media platforms like Google and Facebook are often perceived as the enablers of free speech online and the facilitators of democratic public discourse (Heldt 2022). However, this informational acceleration co-occurred with the decline of democratic processes globally, as Zuboff (2019) and other critical scholars point out. Here, at the end, I analyze similar international developments and I relate them to the Mongolian hybrid media sphere.

First, the relationship between traditional local news media and social media platforms Facebook and Google has resulted in tensions and uncertainties around the world. When social media platforms post snippets of news media and brief media reports, they often do not pay local news organizations. For local news organizations, it is not an easy task to create paywalls to help them recover their costs for producing news. The duopoly domination of social media platforms siphons advertising dollars from local news media they purport to support in local markets (Pickard 2022). Advertisement-deprived media organizations and the immature media market in Mongolia are already engulfed by the global oligopolistic companies, Facebook and Google. Advertisement money put into online sites and social media has exceeded the advertising dollars going to traditional media, according to Maxima Consulting (2017).

Court cases in various countries, from France to Germany and Australia (Royal and Napoli 2022) are creating a ripple effect on news media spheres in many countries involving news organizations and governments, but the outcomes are still too new to summarize. One of the latest legislative efforts in Australia, The News Media Bargaining Code, required the platforms 1) to pay news publishers for showing news snippets and linking to them, 2) to turn in user interaction data, and 3) to inform the publishers about the algorithms that affect rankings and displays of news items (Royal and Napoli 2022). Facebook reacted with a news blackout for a week in Australia in 2021, removing news feeds from Australian users, but the Australian legislation made some concessions for Facebook, allowing it to make license deals with publishers. News organizations, including Australian-based News Corp owned by media baron Rupert Murdock, experienced a big dropout in traffic following Facebook's blackout.

In Mongolia, legislators do not intervene in Facebook and have even collaborated with it to curb political defamation cases, as I discussed in the previous chapters. Even though there has not been a case involving content distribution on Facebook, a legal gap exists in regulating various platforms and providing fair competition conditions among media services.

In 2021, a forerunner case against the Authority for Fair Competition and Consumer Protection of Mongolia brought by Mongol TV[4] asked that the state agency clearly classify the spheres of operation and services among various content providers such as Mongol TV and multichannel operator Univision. Mongol TV, the plaintiff in this civil court case, claimed that the multichannel operator with market power potentially interferes with Mongol TV's audience and data of its viewership. The third party in the case, Univision IPTV, which carries Mongol TV on its internet protocol television and cable network, denied that it has market power. The preliminary civil court denied the request; however, this kind of court case will increase in the near future in relation to the broadcast fund collected from multichannel operators to national broadcasters as written in the Law on Broadcast 2019. This incentivization of content providers with the fund might increase the number of court cases because of the uncertainties in the law that regulates various platforms, content providers, and telecommunications operators.

Second, social media platforms prioritize sensationalized and engagement-inducing content over the veracity and priority of news and curate these news snippets with artificial intelligence and algorithms that are opaque to everyone (Royal and Napoli 2022). Globally, media policies regarding Facebook's roles in public discourse fall into two opposing camps: 1) for restricting Facebook's power in censoring or reporting users, and 2) for holding Facebook responsible for monitoring hateful, unlawful, and defamatory content and curbing disinformation (Green and Tho Le 2022). The former, libertarian view is common in the United States, and the latter, social responsibility view is common in European countries. The Mongolian practice with Facebook seem to veer to the latter, where Facebook collaborates with authority to curb defamatory speech and disinformation, but with one big difference that individuals are responsible in court cases, not Facebook.

Facebook wields great power in this collaboration with authority meaning that Facebook can block or lock out a person on the claim of spreading false information. Mongolia is a politically open country, yet anyone who encounters any defamation on the social network can complain to the police. In 2019, the Mongolian Parliament criminalized the spread of "manifestly false information" (*илт худал мэдээлэл*) on social media in the criminal codes, as I discussed in chapter 4. This kind of power given to market-domineering

4 Ulaanbaatar city Civil Court decision, Jan 15, 2021, accessed https://shuukh.mn/single_case/7460?start_date=&end_date=&id=1&court_cat=3&bb=1

Facebook exacerbates already manifested market failures of the partisan press, paid reports, and extensive nondisclosure agreements in the media. Corruption indexes are high in Mongolia,[5] and media and journalists are threatened by elites who wield political and economic power and sue them for defamation and political disinformation. In chapter 4, I discussed how the highest number of people suing journalists for defamation are government officials, creating chilling effects on journalists and media. This situation leads to a vicious cycle of corruption in Mongolia, while social media networks Facebook and Twitter are protected from being sued for harmful content posted by users.

Facebook reacts and takes down copyrighted materials and bans or removes accounts after hate speech or conspiracy cycles spread (Royal and Napoli 2022). It has been investigated in the US for its invasive tracking of users, its role in far-right group congregation, and for enabling the spread of misinformation and disinformation on its platform. The reach of Facebook in Mongolia shows the extent to which the surveillance technologies track people's private lives, as Zuboff (2019) explains. While it is difficult to show that surveillance capitalism and predictive and behavioral surpluses of Mongolians are being extracted by tech giants, this book documented that people's everyday lives are increasingly "rendered," creating "digital dossiers" for stakeholders of global corporations. These companies sell large numbers of behavioral surpluses to advertisers utilizing the knowledge asymmetry the companies have over users. Like in Facebook's infamous 2016 experiment involving Cambridge Analytica during the elections, in which sixty-one million people participated worldwide, Facebook's experimentation never stops for predictive products. Following the attack on the capitol in the United States on January 6, 2021, the platform's responsibility in local politics and anti-democratization processes and the disruptive effects of social media on local news media have been questioned internationally (Green and Tho Le 2022).

State and corporate surveillance builds extensive dossiers on people using systems like "social scores" in China and national identity cards with fingerprints in Mongolia. Surrender to capitalist and state surveillance by ordinary people leads to even less trust in institutions. Citizen participation in civic life has increasingly been tied to media literacy skills due to the increased influence of media itself on of all processes of social and civic life everywhere in the world. The urgency for laws

5 Transparency International's Corruption Index for Mongolia is thirty-five out of one hundred and the country ranks 110th among 180 countries.

balancing the privacy rights of citizens and the interest of powerful businesses and states is looming large worldwide, indicated by recent regulations, including the GDRP in Europe and NetzDG in Germany. However, relatively new institutions in Mongolia are not well-equipped to deal with dramatic changes in values, identities, markets, and technologies. In a way, Mongolia has been in an interstitial state of transforming from a George Orwellian communist surveillance state to Aldous Huxley's dystopian "brave new world" over the last thirty years. Mongolians joined the global information society, and in order to fully participate they will need to develop a critical and more powerful understanding of all distant and local information.

Work Cited

Billé, Franck. 2015. *Sinophobia: Anxiety, Violence, and the Making of the Mongolian Identity.* University of Hawai'i Press.

Bulag, Uradyn E. 1998. *Nationalism and Hybridity in Mongolia.* Clarendon Press.

Dolgormaa, L. & Kim Kisun. 2023. "The Progress and Changes in Mongolian Diaspora Formation in South Korea" *Mongolian Diaspora. Journal of Mongolian History and Culture.* https://doi.org/10.1515/modi-2021-010104

https://www.degruyter.com/document/doi/10.1515/modi-2021-010104/html

Erdenetuya, D. 2022. *Хятад, Монголын харилцааг гурамсан хөдөлгүүрээр урагшлуулна.* [The relations between Mongolia and China will triple]. News.mn, Nov 30. https://news.mn/r/2608108/.

Fan, Xu. 2022. "Inner Mongolia Readying to Flex Muscles in Film and TV Industries." *China Daily,* July 26. https://www.chinadaily.com.cn/a/202207/26/WS62df8227a310fd2b29e6e74e.html.

Green, Lelia and Viet Tho Le. 2022. "Holding the Line: Responsibility, Digital Citizenship and the Platforms." In *Digital Platform Regulation: Global Perspectives on Internet Governance,* edited by Terry Flew and Fiona R. Martin, 85–111. Palgrave Global Media Policy and Business. Palgrave Macmillan. https://doi.org/10.1007/978-3-030-95220-4_2.

Flew, Terry. 2020. "Globalization, Neo-Globalization and Post-Globalization: The Challenge of Populism and the Return of the National." *Global Media and Communication* 16 (1): 19–39.

Heldt, Amélie. 2022. "EU Digital Services Act: The White Hope of Intermediary Regulation." In *Digital Platform Regulation: Global Perspectives on Internet Governance,* edited by Terry Flew and Fiona Martin, 69–85. Palgrave Global Media Policy and Business. Palgrave Macmillan. https://doi.org/10.1007/978-3-030-95220-4_2.

Kaplonski. Christopher. 2004. *Truth, History and Politics in Mongolia: The Memory of Heroes*. London: Routledge.

Kymlicka, Will and Alan Patten, eds. 2003. *Language Rights and Political Theory.* Oxford University Press.

Maxima Consulting. 2017. Television Audience Research Summary [Телевиз үзэлтийн судалгааны нэгдсэн тайлан]. https://maxima.mn/2017-tam-tailan.

Maxima Consulting. 2020. Television Audience Research Summary [Телевиз үзэлтийн судалгааны нэгдсэн тайлан]. https://maxima.mn/2020-tam-tailan.

May, Stephen. 2012. *Language and Minority Rights: Ethnicity, Nationalism and the Politics of Language*. 2nd ed. Routledge.

Parliament of Mongolia. 2015. Соёлын Тухай Хуульд Нэмэлт Оруулах Тухай [Addendum to The Law on Culture]. https://www.parliament.mn/laws/15735/.

Pickard, Victor. 2022. "Can Journalism Survive in the Age of Platform Monopolies? Confronting Facebook's Negative Externalities." In *Digital Platform Regulation: Global Perspectives on Internet Governance*, edited by Terry Flew and Fiona Martin, 23–41. Palgrave Global Media Policy and Business. Palgrave Macmillan. https://doi.org/10.1007/978-3-030-95220-4_2.

PIM. 2022. *Mongolian Media Today.* Ulaanbaatar: PIM.

"Racism in Mongolia." DW, April 17, 2012. https://www.dw.com/en/rampant-racism-a-growing-problem-in-mongolia/a-15888287.

Rossabi, Morris. 2021. "Mongolia in 2020: Less COVID, Lots of Problems." *Asian Survey* 61 (1): 43–48.

Royal, Asa and Philip M. Napoli. 2022. "Platforms and the Press: Regulatory Interventions to Address an Imbalance of Power." In *Digital Platform Regulation: Global Perspectives on Internet Governance*, edited by Terry Flew and Fiona R. Martin, 43–67. Palgrave Global Media Policy and Business. Palgrave Macmillan. https://doi.org/10.1007/978-3-030-95220-4_3.

Shih, Gerry. 2020. "Chinese Authorities Face Widespread Anger in Inner Mongolia After Requiring Mandarin-Language Classes." *The Washington Post*, April 31. https://www.washingtonpost.com/world/asia_pacific/chinese-authorities-face-widespread-anger-in-inner-mongolia-after-requiring-mandarin-language-classes/2020/08/31/3ba5a938-eb5b-11ea-bd08-1b10132b458f_story.html.

"Россия и Монголия могут нарастить товарооборот до $5 млрд к 2026 году" [Trade Between Russia and Mongolia Will Increase to $ 5 Billion by 2026]. TASS, May 27, 2022. Accessed Jan 2, 2023. https://tass.ru/ekonomika/14757167.

Taylor, Emely. 2016. "The Privatization of Human Rights: Illusion of Consent, Automation and Neutrality." CIGI. https://www.cigionline.org/sites/default/files/gcig_no24_web_2.pdf.

Trenz, Hans-Jörg. 2007. "Reconciling Diversity and Unity: Language Minorities and European Integration." *Ethnicities* 7 (2): 162–85.

UN General Assembly, Resolution 217A (III), "Universal Declaration of Human Rights," December 10, 1948, https://www.un.org/en/development/desa/population/migration/generalassembly/docs/globalcompact/A_RES_217(III).pdf

Zuboff, Shoshana. 2019. *The Age of Surveillance Capitalism: The Fight for a Human Future at the New Frontier of Power.* New York: Public Affairs.

Acknowledgments

I must acknowledge the contributions of many people without whom I would not been able to finish this book. I would like to thank my series editors, Drs. Franck Billé and Caroline Humphrey for believing in and guiding me throughout the project. Loretta Lou at the Amsterdam University Press was instrumental in carrying the project from the proposal to peer reviews and production stages. I would like to also thank the reviewers of the manuscript for helping me improve the book.

This book would not have been realized without support from the fellowships of the William J. Fulbright US Scholar Program and the American Center for Mongolian Studies (ACMS). This support allowed me to conduct fieldwork in Mongolia. Host institutions, The National University, the Open Society Foundations, and the American Center for Mongolian Studies, provided me with incredible support during the fieldwork. I would like to thank Sophya Yang at the Fulbright, P. Erdenejargal, D. Enkhtsetsed, and A. Gerelmaa at the Open Society Foundations, Ch. Lodoiravsal, Sh. Mendbayar, Tumenbayar Saya-Erdene, B. Bold-Erdene, T. Unersiakhan, B. Naranbaatar, B. Tuvshintur, D. Iderjargal, N. Ariunzaya, B. Bayarmaa, and Badamdash Dashdavaa at the National University, and David Dettman and B. Baigalmaa at the American Center for Mongolian Studies.

I acknowledge the invaluable insights and contributions of many interlocutors, including internet founder Dangaasürengiin Enkhbat, Naranjargal Khashkhuu at Globe International Center, Munkhmandakh Myagmar at the Press Institute, Ya. Khishigsuren and Z. Enkhjargal at Maxima Consulting, Ya. Dashdorj at the Technology University, and journalists Budragchaa, Tsoojchuluuntsetseg, and Purevsuren.

I would also like to thank colleagues in my home institution, Southern Illinois University Edwardsville: Department Chair Musonda Kapatamoyo, Deans Greg Budzban and Jen Rehg for their support during the difficult COVID–19 pandemic. The support of the writing group members, Drs. Saba Fatima, Allison Rheinheld, and Jessica DeSpain helped me. Several colleagues in other institutions, Paulette Kilmer at Toledo University, Poul Nielsen at Aarhus, and Patrick Murphy at Temple supported me in obtaining fellowships and realizing the book's ideas.

This project would not have been realized without the love and support of my spouse John Borczon, daughter Tsolmon Lkhagvasuren, and her partner Jeff Perez. My spouse John has been the first reader and the insightful editor of all chapters. I am blessed by my late parents, Tsevegjav Norjmaa and Damchaa Baasanjav, and would like to thank my siblings, Oyunbileg, Maskhbadrakh, Erdenebileg, and Ganbolor for their support during the difficult times.

Index

For Product Safety Concerns and Information please contact our EU representative GPSR@taylorandfrancis.com Taylor & Francis Verlag GmbH, Kaufingerstraße 24, 80331 München, Germany

Batch number: 10725973

Printed by Printforce, the Netherlands